FIGHTER LEADER

By the same author:
DOUBLE MISSION: RAF Fighter Ace and SOE Agent –
Manfred Czernin

FIGHTER LEADER

The Story of
Wing Commander Ian Gleed
DSO, DFC, Croix de Guerre

by

Norman L.R. Franks

WILLIAM KIMBER · LONDON

First published in 1978 by
WILLIAM KIMBER & CO. LIMITED
Godolphin House, 22a Queen Anne's Gate,
London, SW1H 9AE

© Norman L.R. Franks, 1978
ISBN 0 7183 01064

Photoset by
Specialised Offset Services Limited, Liverpool
and printed and bound in Great Britain by
REDWOOD BURN LIMITED
Trowbridge & Esher

Contents

List of Illustrations

Maps

Acknowledgements

I am grateful for the generous help and assistance from many quarters during my research for this book. My special thanks go to Doctor Daphne Gleed MRCS LRCP for her willing co-operation and her enthusiasm. Also to Mr Edward 'Teddy' Denman.

From Ian Gleed's schooldays and youth I am indebted to Mr J.B. Bell MBE BA, Bursar of Epsom College, Mr W.E. Radcliffe and Mr S.A. Weare, two of Gleed's schoolmasters. Also the following former students of Epsom College. Vice-Admiral Sir Peter Compston KCB, Doctor Ronald C.R. Gethen MRCS LRCP, and Surgeon Rear Admiral Cyril L.T. McClintock CB OBE. In addition my thanks to Mr W J.R. Medlock and Mr Raymond Mays.

To those who knew Gleed while serving with the Royal Air Force, my thanks for their recollections go to Air Chief Marshal Sir Harry Broadhurst GCB KBE DSO DFC AFC, Air Chief Marshal Sir Frederick Rosier GCB CBE DSO, Air Commodore James B. Coward AFC, Wing Commander Roland Beamont CBE DSO DFC FRAES, Wing Commander Christopher F. Currant DSO DFC, Wing Commander Neville F. Duke DSO OBE DFC AFC, Squadron Leader D.C. Usher DFC DFM, and Squadron Leader Laurence Thorogood DFC.

I am also more than grateful to my good friend Chaz Bowyer for his help, advice and original research notes. Also to the Executors of the late Hector Bolitho for permission to quote from *A Penguin in the Eyrie* and to the Executors of the late W. Somerset Maugham for permission to quote from *Strictly Personal*.

The staff of the following establishments have my thanks: Air Historical Branch, Ministry of Defence; RAF Museum, Hendon; and the Public Records Office.

Finally to my wife Kate, for checking the manuscript, and for being there. Also to my two sons. May their courage be shown in ways far removed from war.

CHAPTER ONE

Early Life

Ian Richard Gleed was born at the family home, Brighton Lodge, Long Lane, Finchley in North London, on 3 July 1916. He was the second child of Doctor Seymour Richard Gleed MD and his wife Florence.

Doctor Gleed had been in general practice since 1909 but in 1915 had offered his services to his country, receiving a commission in the Royal Army Medical Corps. He served throughout the war, seeing many harrowing sights on the battlefields of Flanders. On one occasion he was gassed when attending casualties in a pill-box; his wife received a telegram that he had been badly wounded, but fortunately her husband sent his own telegram soon afterwards saying he was well and would soon be home. In 1918 he received a Mention in Despatches for his work; the certificate was signed on behalf of Field Marshal Haig by the Minister of War, Mr Winston Churchill – the man who would inspire a nation in the world's second great conflict with Germany. In that conflict the son of Doctor Seymour Gleed was destined to make his mark.

At the end of the Great War, Doctor Gleed returned to general practice, and the family home and surgery moved to Edenvale, 38 Ballards Lane, Finchley in 1919. Ian and his older sister Daphne enjoyed a happy childhood even though as youngsters they were constantly aware that they must be seen and not heard in a house in which their father's busy surgery was situated, especially as their day nursery, ruled by their Nanny, was above the surgery and waiting room. For the two children, especially to a vigorous and lively boy and his particular friends, this must have been a difficult thing to do.

Ian Gleed's education began at Tenterden Preparatory School where one particular friend was W.J.R. 'Reg' Medlock, who was to play, by a strange twist of circumstances, an unusual part in the final chapter of his young friend's life. After Tenterden, Gleed went to Epsom College in Surrey during 1928, when he was twelve years old. At Epsom he went to Fayrer House, where his house master was the Reverend Michael William Robertson MA, late of Trinity College Dublin, whose nickname was 'Pomp'.

One of his tutors while in the Junior House, situated in the College's Newsom building, was Mr S.A. Weare – a mathematics master who recalls:

> ... I had the pleasure of taking Form 1 ... I say pleasure as the periods were five minutes shorter than normal and Form 1 consisted of eight boys only. I remember Ian very clearly – short but stocky – regularly seventh of eight in form order! He was always very friendly and asked a lot of questions. I remember that he acted in a house play and was prominent as the language (for those days) was pretty vivid.

Although the young Gleed was regularly seventh in this class, Mr Weare remembers that it was a boy by the name of D – who was always eighth. D – was constantly breaking his glasses so the side pieces had to be tied together round the back of his head to prevent them from falling off.

Another master who remembers Gleed was Mr W.E. Radcliffe who as a very junior master at the time had rooms in Newsom Buildings. Although Mr Radcliffe does not recall Gleed particularly well – 'he was not a boy to excite notice' – he does recall a college play: 'Once when I produced an Eugene O'Neill play Ian learnt its full original text instead of the expurgated version which we used.'

Mr Radcliffe recollects that Gleed was one of a group of boys, Ian Huntley-Wood and Peter Compston being among them. All three would fly in World War Two. Huntley-Wood, later a squadron leader in the RAFVR flying with Bomber Command, like Gleed was decorated and also destined to die in 1943.[1] Compston flew with the Fleet Air Arm, survived the war and retired from the Royal Navy as an admiral and became President of the Old

[1] Huntley-Wood flew Avro Manchesters with 207 Squadron, winning the DFC.

Epsonians. Sir Peter Compston recalls:

> Looking back I think we all three had one thing in common so far as work was concerned – we were bone idle and must have been the despair of those unfortunate masters who manfully attempted to educate us. On the playing field and in other outdoor pursuits we fared rather better, and we all boxed for the school. We were also the sort of 'thugs' who captured prisoners on Field Days in the Officers Training Corps. We were all three of us intended to practise medicine or so our families hopefully wished but fate and Hitler decided otherwise.

Gleed's and Huntley-Wood's distinguished war records do not surprise Peter Compston at all. They were both, he remembers, gifted with an enormous amount of guts and initiative. The three of them were usually up to some prank or other, one being the evening they 'borrowed' Mr Radcliffe's car when all of them should have been attending a lecture on Piltdown Man. They were all soundly thrashed for their non-attendance but they managed to return the car in one piece and this escapade was never discovered.

Compston and Gleed were destined to meet again after leaving Epsom, at Number 8 Flying Training School at Montrose in Scotland, where Gleed was one term ahead of his friend: 'It was generally agreed that he [Gleed] was one of the most outstanding aviators there, and was a natural fighter pilot.'

At Montrose Gleed had a small Ford motorcar and he and Compston thought nothing of driving to London and back for a weekend, quite a trip in those days but no doubt well worth it. Compston remembers that Gleed was on the whole a bit of a loner, and one of his main pursuits at the end of the flying day was to set off in his car with a rifle and do a bit of poaching at which he was adept.

On one occasion at Epsom Gleed and his two associates built a bonfire into which they put a blank cartridge at a moment when they had very carefully calculated its explosion would coincide with the arrival of their housemaster. The plot failed, however, and they had to accept the usual penalty.

Gleed also gained some degree of fame on his own account. There were the two McClintock brothers at Epsom, Jon who was head of Fayrer in 1932 and who later took holy orders and became a canon, and his brother Cyril. Cyril, later Surgeon Rear Admiral, recalls:

> The story that sticks in my mind was that he was the only boy known to have succeeded in seeing the Derby [at Epsom Downs racecourse]. In those days of iron railings and seclusion, roll calls were held at uncertain times on Derby Day to prevent boys going up onto the Downs and being contaminated by the wicked crowds. This required ingenuity, stamina and a well breached accomplice with a car.

This story also remains in the memory of another student at Epsom, Ronald Gethen. As Gethen confirms, the College boys were always closely closeted during the Derby Week, especially on Derby Day. The boys were 'gated' and as McClintock says, snap roll calls were made to ensure all the boys were within the College boundaries. Even if a boy was taking a bath he had to report to his housemaster.

On this particular Derby Day Gleed was determined to see the big race and just strolled out of the College. Rather than a fast car, he probably just walked up onto the Downs which were only about a mile and a half away. The roll call was made, just before the time of the big race, and soon everyone was fully aware that Gleed was missing. Pomp Robertson left clear instructions that Gleed was to report to him instantly he reappeared, so all the boys knew Gleed would be for it. Eventually Gleed did reappear and was quickly brought to the Reverend Robertson.

'Where have you been, Gleed?' asked Robertson, 'You were not in attendance when the roll was called?'

'Oh, didn't Miss Bailey tell you?' replied Gleed, all wide eyed and innocent. 'She invited me to have tea with her? I assumed that as I was with her I need not report.' Miss Bailey was the school matron and Gleed knew, as most of the boys knew, that Robertson could not stand the matron. Gleed took a chance that Robertson would not check his story, thereby having to actually speak to the lady. Robertson was extremely angry that matron should have the temerity to ask Gleed to tea without letting him know. Much to the surprise of the other boys it was a smiling Gleed that emerged from

Robertson's study clearly unharmed, unchastised and he soon became something of a local hero.

Ronald Gethen, later to become a doctor and who served as a surgeon lieutenant commander in the Royal Navy in WW2, was senior to Gleed at Epsom and he also remembers a far less heroic episode in Gleed's schooldays. Gleed slept in a small eight-boy dormitory and Ronnie Gethen was the prefect in charge of this dorm. Because of his position his bed was located right by the door of the room, his head being only a few inches from the door handle. One night he heard a slight sound and was instantly wide awake, seeing in the gloom the unmistakable figure of the diminutive Gleed in the act of creeping out. Gethen followed him, finding a fully clothed Gleed, clearly not going to the ablutions and equally clearly up to no good. He was taken to the housemaster where, under questioning, it was revealed that as a dare, he had been on his way to Epsom. The object of his visit was to break into a house and as proof of having carried out the deed had to bring back an object taken from it. On being searched some tools were discovered and this time it was not a smiling nor an unharmed Gleed that stiffly emerged from Robertson's study.

Doctor Gethen also recalls that, in his mind Gleed was a rather scruffy little individual, not overliked and he was usually thumped (or kicked) by some of the boys just because he was there. Being on the small side probably made this easier but it obviously did not affect him as it might well have done. Gethen, as much as anyone, was later to be utterly amazed to read of Gleed's success as a fighter pilot and especially surprised at his leadership qualities which had made not the slightest sign of emergence while he had been at Epsom College.

The College records do not note Gleed as receiving any prizes or as being in any of the College sporting teams but he did enjoy sport. He boxed and liked to play tennis and while away from Epsom, played for the Finchley Rugby Club during the winter months. In 1934 he won a tankard for boxing and due to his height and weight was dubbed a 'paper-weight!' He had little desire to be a success at his studies while at Epsom, probably doing just sufficient to get by. As Mr Radcliffe sums up: 'He had no pretensions to or any desire for an academic success while at Epsom.'

Yet he did not forget his old school when he left and joined the Royal Air Force. In 1940, soon after his return from France, he visited Epsom and chatted with Mr Weare about some of his experiences. On another occasion, this same master was disturbed by an aeroplane flying overhead late one evening.

One dark night a plane kept diving over the College – obviously an Old Boy – so I went out into the open and with my torch, a powerful one, shone it at the plane and signalled in morse 'Go away'. To my surprise a signal came back from his tail and he cleared off. I was unable to read the signal as I did not expect it. Later I saw Ian and asked him if he was the pilot – he said, 'Yes, I couldn't get down at Croydon until they cleared the remains of a plane which had crashed there, so I decided to occupy the time over the College!'

CHAPTER TWO

The Explorer

While at Epsom College in his late teens, Ian Gleed became an active member of the PSES – the Public Schools Exploring Society. In this way, this 'sometimes horrible little boy' gained some respect from a few of his fellow pupils.

The Society had been formed in 1932 by Surgeon-Commander G. Murray Levick RN, its first trial expedition going to Lapland. Murray Levick took eight boys from public schools, and spent a month in virgin forest land under pioneering conditions. Whilst there they made short journeys using compass headings, of two or three days' duration, the party carrying their own food and camping equipment. During their expedition they logged meteorological observations, made records of flora and fauna studied and added several items of interest to existing maps. This inaugural trip proved the feasibility of such expeditions and encouraged Levick to formulate and expand his ideas for future expeditions of a larger size.

Murray Levick, or the 'Admiral' as everyone called him, was more than qualified as the Society's founder and leader. He had been a member of Scott's tragic Antarctic Expedition in 1910, in which he acted as both medical officer and zoologist. Afterwards he had further adventures in the Antarctic regions before he returned to England in 1913, and studied in some depth the social habits of the penguin. His subsequent book on these fascinating creatures was considered a classic on the subject. During the First World War he had served with the Royal Navy. After the war he had gone into private medical practice but had to sacrifice this when his Exploring Society idea really took off in a big way. However, he managed to continue in medicine as a consultant to several hospitals and was a member of the London University Advisory Committee on Physical Education.

His thoughts and views upon which the PSES was founded were that modern youth in the 1930's was in danger of becoming soft due to the luxuries of modern living, of losing its appreciation of physical endeavour and of losing the art of fighting for its existence with Nature. From these simple but fundamental beliefs the Society flourished in the immediate pre-war years, its first patron-in-chief being His Royal Highness the Prince of Wales.

The following summer, 1933, a second expedition to Finnish Lapland was arranged, but this time the party consisted of Murray Levick, three assistant leaders, a doctor and thirty schoolboys. If the 1932 expedition had proved the feasibility of the scheme, the 1933 trip was designed to test fully the equipment for future years and to discover what distance a team of picked public schoolboys could cover over tractless forest, carrying their own food etc: Ian Gleed, at seventeen years of age, was one of two boys who went from Epsom on a purely voluntary basis, the other being C.E.A. Towne.

Amid much cheering and not a little publicity the party left King's Cross Railway Station at 10.15 am on Wednesday, 2 August, being seen off by Admiral Sir Lionel Halsey GCMG KCMG KCIE KCVO, one of the Society's patrons. Travelling to Hull the party boarded the SS *Arcturus* of the Finnish Line and sailed for Copenhagen. Following a short stay in this city where many of the boys spent an evening at the famous Tivoli gardens, then the world's greatest fun-fair, they sailed again, this time for Sweden.

The party disembarked at Helsinki on the morning of 7 August and after depositing their gear at the Hotel Karelia were taken on a conducted tour of the city by the Finnish Scholastic Travel Bureau. Many of the boys also took the chance of a Finn Bath (the Sauna of today). Having changed into bathing trunks they were directed to go to the hot rooms. Passing an inviting swimming pool on the way, some of the boys dived in, much to the horror of those Finns already in the water. It was a prerequisite of the baths that they should have first sweated out the dirt from their bodies before plunging into the pool.

Two days later, kitted out and looking every bit a very workmanlike party they entrained at Helsinki's main railway station for the four hundred mile journey northwards. Even at this early stage the boys' spirits were high. Some soon found their way onto the roofs of the carriages while others discovered a matronly Finnish lady who offered to sew a button back onto a boy's coat sleeve. Apparently several boys then proceeded to cut off various buttons to enjoy the pleasure of them being sewn back on. Another attraction upon leaving various railway stations along the journey was to wait until the last possible moment before climbing aboard. As the stations had no raised platforms as in England, the train had running boards fitted. Several boys managed to run along by the train for some distance beyond the stations before having at last to leap onto the running boards, but this dangerous pastime was quickly discovered and stopped.

The town of Oula, a port in the north west of Finland, ended their train journey but they continued on by lorry for a further two hundred miles over roads of sand, rock, rubble and grass! At Lake Kallunkijarvi they transferred their $1\frac{1}{2}$ tons of equipment into some small boats to cross the two mile expanse of water; their Base Camp area was situated about five miles further on, on the bank of the Oulankajoki River – approximately ten miles south of the Arctic Circle and just thirty miles from the Russian border.

The first exploration parties went out on the morning of 13 August, Gleed was one of an eleven-man team headed by Mr G.J. Hamilton, known as 'Flags', and including 'The Doc', Doctor Allen Crockford MC, the medical officer. Gleed and the team journeyed up the right-hand fork of the Oulankajoki which ran through a canyon carved out by ice when a glacier flowed down the valley. They fished the river which produced some welcome trout to augment their spartan food supplies. Their first planned destination was Savinajoki Lake which they reached safely although four members of the party had badly blistered feet after struggling along a precipitous route littered with rocks and dead trees.

Leaving these four at the lake to fish, Flags and the rest, including Gleed, moved on to explore further before returning to the lake when evening came. That night bears could be heard in the forest and some excitement was generated when an adder was killed in the camp area. The next morning the fit members of the party proceeded up the Savinajoki River and by the time they returned to the campsite in the evening a total of sixteen miles had been covered. They returned to the Base Camp the next day, intact and with note pads filled with facts, sightings and recordings.

After these trial expeditions, the group was split into other parties, the main one going with Murray Levick north for six days, returning on the twelfth day. Gleed was not chosen as part of this 'Long March', but he went out on two shorter journeys. The first was for a five day trek followed by a second of two and a half days to meet the returning Long March party. The Five Day March proved of interest; the team was led by Captain W.J. Pearce, the executive officer and known as 'The Bosun'. Having seen off the Long March group, the Bosun led his party eight miles north to Lake Elijarvi. Much of the journey was through some nasty swampland which made progress slow and hard. Their target the next day was Lake Hangasjarvi just over six miles to the north-east, giving the boys an opportunity to do some practical map-reading plus some very necessary intelligent guesswork. By the third day, several of the party had developed raging colds and so they decided on an easy day but were plagued by hordes of midges until the evening. The party marched to Lake Ouliolampi on day four. They reached it safely, and were rewarded with a beautiful view of the lake, river and waterfall from a hilltop above Kiutakongas where Gleed and some of the others took some photographs. Two of Gleed's photos were later used to help illustrate a book written by Levick on the 1933 expedition. They show a keen sense of composition rather than just taking 'snap-shots'. The party, having covered its roughly circular route, arrived back at base that evening.

With the return of the Long March party, the main objectives of the Expedition had been completed. It was now September and nearly time to journey home. However, Murray Levick offered to take any of the boys who wished to go to Kylakoski about twelve miles away by land and water, to shoot the rapids there. Gleed, always to the fore, was one of the ten who volunteered to go, starting out on the 3rd. They stayed the night at a farm and the next day trekked to the rapids where each boy in turn shot the rapids in a canoe.

Base Camp was broken two days later and the group sadly returned to Helsinki and home aboard the SS *Ilmatar*. On the ship was a contingent of the Black Watch who had been in Helsinki for British Week so it was a very noisy send off by the Finns, while the Black Watch band played 'Auld Lang Syne'.

All the boys returned wiser, not to say more muscular, but had adequately proved to their leader that modern youth was far from soft.

The following summer Ian Gleed again volunteered as a member of the PSES party; this time the Society went to Newfoundland. For this expedition apart from Murray Levick as leader, there were five assistant leaders including 'Doc' Crockford and a historian, Dennis Clarke, a Fleet Street journalist who was to write a book on the expedition (*Public School Explorers in Newfoundland*, Putnam 1935). The number of boys was increased to 46. Six of these had, like Gleed, been on the 1933 Lapland trip and one of these had been on both the 1932 and 1933 expeditions (D.F. Pearl of Ardingly). Captain C.A. Carkeet-James RA – 'The Mate' – was again second-in-command.

This year the scene of departure was Euston Railway Station and again it was Sir Lionel Halsey that saw them all off that August day. Arriving at Liverpool they boarded the SS *Nova Scotia* and amid photographers' flashing light bulbs the ship was cheered away from the dock to nose its way out towards the Atlantic via the Irish Sea. The crossing took five days during which every cricket ball aboard was eventually hit into the sea soon followed by every tennis ball lost during games of stoolball.

The coast of Newfoundland came into sight shortly after lunch on 9 August. Docking at St John's the party entrained for Grand Falls where they arrived the next day. After a short stay, being royally entertained by the inhabitants, the party travelled by motor launch and trucks forty-odd miles inland to a lumberman's camp known as Thirty-Mile depot. At this last outpost they ate and enjoyed a lumberman's meal of bully beef, potatoes and baked beans, followed by several large fruit tarts.

The Expedition's base camp was ten miles further on, and the tents were pitched that evening beside the site's river – Great Rattling Brook. After establishing this base camp, the main party moved forward to establish a depot further inland from where serious exploration was planned to take place. Each young man had to carry 52 pounds of food and equipment over rough forest land aided only by compass and highly suspect maps. Much of the land over which the PSES boys would spend the next weeks was completely unexplored; only very early pioneers had made approximate locations of several rivers, lakes and high ground. On the journey open ground was sparse, huge belts of trees had to be navigated and trails had to be 'blazed' by cutting pieces of bark from the tree trunks along the way. Their main objective was to discover the head waters of the Gander River and when eventually they came upon a river they thought initially it was the Gander though this later proved incorrect.

They established Depot 1 at this point, but now realised that this river could not possibly be the Gander. The group now split into two groups, one to survey and explore the immediate area and to discover the Gander, the second, like the Lapland trip, to go on a long trek into the interior. Murray Levick again led the Long March boys, and Carkeet-James took charge of the depot party. Gleed remained with the depot party.

Taking stock of their food supplies, the depot party added to this supply by fishing sorties in, what they had now called the Depot River. By revising their calculations and estimations they believed the Gander to be only a few miles further on and guessed that they would soon discover it during their planned traversing forays. Traversing is a technical name for making a journey on a compass heading during which all the physical features encountered to the immediate left and right of the line are noted down in a book. After each traversing party returned their findings were transferred and added to an embryo map which gradually began to take shape under the expert hands of Captain Carkeet-James. The traversing parties found several new lakes and rivers; while all this was going on, the Doc took a party south-east to establish Depot 2 which they located by a lake they named as Upper Mallard Lake. Then all those left at Depot 1 also moved to Depot 2 to explore its environs. It was from here that a large river, undoubtedly the Gander, was found. At this point where they discovered their own Depot River flowed into the Gander, Depot 3 was set up.

Gleed, meantime, during one traversing sortie had found 'his' river. He located this new river north of Depot River and it was widely traversed. It became known as Gleed's River shortly afterwards due to an adventure which happened to Gleed and which was a feature of the whole expedition.

The day following the discovery of this river by Gleed, was spent in moving equipment from Depot 2 to Depot 3. Carkeet-James left Gleed and G.C. Glegg (of Eastbourne College) at Depot 2; Gleed remained in charge, due no doubt to his previous expedition experience. At Depot 2 Gleed was to await the return of a party who had gone out to locate and map a ridge of hills (this group was called the Middle Ridge Party) and then upon their arrival they would all track down to Depot 3.

At Depot 3, the other members took up their various tasks, one of which was the ever important task of catching fish. No news came from Depot 2 but this only suggested that the Middle Ridge Party had not yet reached Gleed and Glegg. However, all was not well as Glegg soon announced upon his breathless arrival at Depot 3.

Glegg quickly related the grim news to those members he found at Depot 3 that Gleed had been missing for three days. Whilst awaiting the Middle Ridge Party Gleed's desire to complete the traverse of 'his' river overcame the Society's instilled discipline. Wearing only a shirt, trousers and plimsolls he had left Glegg at Depot 2. It was completely against orders to move into the forests alone but he obviously thought he could safely reach his river, complete the traverse, and return well before nightfall. He left the camp at mid-day and Glegg had no cause to be concerned until his failure to reappear that evening. Even then it could easily be that Gleed had merely misjudged his return time and had bedded himself down for the night and would undoubtedly walk in the next morning grinning sheepishly all over his face. When he did not appear, his lone companion was put onto the horns of a dilemma.

Glegg had three alternatives open to him. Firstly he could himself go after Gleed in the hope of finding him, the chances of which might well prove slim. He might also lose himself and therefore endanger both of their lives. Secondly he could await the expected return of the Middle Ridge Party so as to enlist their help in a search. Or, thirdly, he could make his way to Depot 3 for the certain help of the members there. If, of course, he left Depot 2, he might miss the Ridge Party and he only had a rough idea of Depot 3's location as Gleed had been given the route, not him. Even if he tried to reach Depot 3 by the time he got there – if he got there – Gleed would, without proper clothing, food etc, be on his last legs. Finally he decided to await the arrival of the Ridge Party but with growing anxiety waited in vain for two days. This left him with little choice but to strike out for Depot 3, which luckily he found and reached in a day's fast march.

By the time Carkeet-James was aware of Gleed's plight, he had been lost for over three days with no food and armed only with a knife. It would take Carkeet-James and the others a day to reach the locality of Gleed's disappearance and although Gleed was well known by the whole group as 'of stout heart and stockily built' he would by that time be completely exhausted. Carkeet-James also had to take into account the possibility of Gleed having injured himself. Perhaps even now he was lying somewhere in the forest with a broken leg, or even unconscious. How would they find him then?

Base Camp was a good three days' march from Depot 3 so help from that direction had to be discounted. By the time assistance came from there, Gleed would have been lost for around ten days, and by then it would be no good at all. Carkeet-James with seven boys set out with five days' supplies to try and locate Gleed by trying to discover where and how he had become lost.

They reached Gleed's River by evening and called out for Gleed up and down the river until they were exhausted. The following morning the search began again, the party spreading out into a line in order to cover a larger area of forest and swampland, calling out Gleed's name in unison every five minutes. They examined the more evil-looking swamps and bogs intently, expecting to find Gleed's hat if the worst had occurred, floating on the top.

It was W.E. Nixon (of Malvern School) who put forward the most likely theory behind Gleed's disappearance. Gleed had known that his river flowed into Depot River and he had probably traversed down it with the intention of turning back to Depot 2 up Depot River when he reached its estuary. However, if he had overlooked the junction and continued down Depot River, still thinking he was on his river he would soon be lost when finally striking out across country to where he thought Depot 2 would be. It might easily be done as the junction in question occurred at a small lake which, if walked around away from Depot River's entrance to it, this entrance could easily be missed. On reaching the exit from the lake, which was actually the continuance of the main Depot River, it could be mistakenly thought to be the Gleed River still flowing towards the estuary.

The search went on. Gleed had now been missing for five days, and Carkeet-James decided to search for two more days, rest one day, then return to Base Camp. By that time there would be little chance of doing anything other than search for Ian Gleed's body. Then H.A. Buxton (of Chillon) spotted a piece of paper under a pile of rock which read: 'River traversed from source, I.R. Gleed, PSES'.

This proved Nixon's theory as correct for they found it some way down Depot River, establishing beyond doubt that Gleed believed completely that he was still on his river. It was probably here that he had gone into the forest, heading, or so he thought, in the direction of Depot 2.

They continued looking but they felt little hope of finding him alive. After a fruitless day they reached Depot 2, packed Gleed's kit and prepared to leave next morning for Base Camp to break the news to the members there.

That evening as the tired searchers rested, rain pouring down

Gleed's River

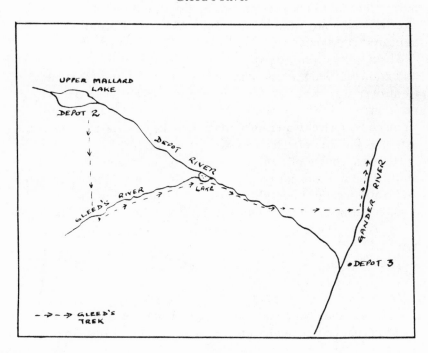

outside, the tent flap suddenly opened and there stood Gleed, soaked from head to foot but still very much alive. He was greeted royally and thought to be truly back from the dead. Gleed then had to relate his story to everyone. As Nixon had theorised, Gleed had become lost within twenty-four hours having moved along Depot River without realising he had left his river.

'I had,' he related to the expedition's historian, Dennis Clarke, 'an extraordinary feeling of danger just before I realised I really was lost. For some absurd reason I felt as though a bear was going to jump on me at any moment.'

He found the ground was rising when it should have been descending into the valley from whence he had just come. Expecting to strike Depot River and with now no sign of water whatsoever, he began to get worried. Later he found a smaller river just as it began to rain and following this he came to a larger river which he took to be the Gander. As the sky darkened he took shelter beneath a fallen tree and covered himself with birch bark but in extreme discomfort from dripping foliage, and animal noises from the forest, he was unable to sleep. He was pestered by mosquitoes and had one hand so badly bitten it swelled to such a size he could not move or bend it. At around midnight a lynx appeared and eyed him suspiciously but then sheered off.

The next morning, guessing correctly that he was on the Gander and knowing Depot 3 was somewhere along its banks, the question to answer was, was it upstream or downstream from his present position? He was desperately hungry but by drinking and filling his stomach with river water he managed to alleviate the pangs to some extent. A few, but only a few, wild berries also helped.

His only course of action was to walk upstream for four hours and if Depot 3 did not come into view he would retrace his steps and travel for four hours downstream. If still nothing was found he would continue down the Gander to the sea, an estimated 60 miles away. At first light he left a note under a rock, building a cairn on top.

The note read:

Public Schools Exploring Society
I am lost somewhere on the Gander. I have no food. I am going to march for four hours upstream, and unless I find anything I

shall attempt to march to the sea. I think I can live for five days. Please leave food on this rock.

This he signed, dated and timed. The rain had stopped and a warming sun cheered him somewhat. At around 10 am he found himself suddenly very tired and beginning to stagger. He was, although he probably did not realise it, close to collapse. He forced himself on and with still no signs of Depot 3, resolved to turn back at the next estuary. Then, as he neared a bend in the river, saw above the trees some smoke rising into the still air. He made the bend and saw in the distance some movement on the riverbank near the smoke. It was a man who moved away as he watched him and the smoke too began to disappear.

Summoning up his last reserves of strength he ran forward, shouting. The location where the smoke had been was still some distance off and in fact the men there were just breaking camp and were about to move off when they heard his call. Gleed saw other people appear and one man ran towards him. It was the Middle Ridge Party who had in fact decided not to go to Depot 2 and were just starting for Base Camp. If Gleed had been only a few minutes later in coming into sight of their dying fire smoke, they would have moved off and he would have turned back. If he would have been able to make the sixty mile trek to the sea is highly doubtful.

The Middle Ridge Party gave him food and he then rested for a few hours before marching off with them to Base Camp which took 1½ days. Following a night's rest at Base Camp, Gleed felt much better. He then walked the twenty miles to Thirty-Mile Depot to borrow some boots, returned, and with three companions and a gun (he was determined not to go hungry or face wild animals again) set off for Depot 3. He then went on to Depot 2 where he found the search party at last.

When Murray Levick finally returned from his Long March and heard of the Gleed business he was extremely cross with him, pointing out that but for his lucky encounter with the Middle Ridge Party who should not have been where he found them, he would have undoubtedly perished.

'Nevertheless, I think that Gleed's self-possession when lost and his general conduct after that,' said Levick later, 'especially in marching so promptly back to the Depot to relieve the anxiety of

Carkeet-James and the others, to a large extent cancels out his original offence.'

Thus Gleed survived and returned to England an older and a wiser young man. He was quite obviously not destined to perish unsung in the wilderness of Newfoundland.

CHAPTER THREE

The Sailor

In 1934, Doctor Gleed bought a bungalow at High Cliff, Burlington Drive, Beltinge, near Herne Bay, Kent, which was used as a retreat from the pressures of North London, which the family retained and used for twenty-one years. It was here that Ian Gleed became interested in sailing, soon joining the Herne Bay Sailing Club.

Like most youngsters he began 'messing about' in small sailing dinghies at weekends or during school holidays. By 1937, when he was approaching his twenty-first birthday, he was a very keen and competent sailor and yachtsman. Sailing became his second love, after flying, and during his flying training it was a useful diversion and helped his navigation. His parents, delighted at his sailing prowess, bought for him on his twenty-first birthday, a 14 foot sailing dinghy, the *Spindrift*, which became his pride and delight. Hardly an opportunity to travel down to Herne Bay and sail his boat was missed and only a month after owning the *Spindrift*, Gleed won first prize at the West Cliff Regatta in the sailing dinghies' class.

Ian Gleed took part in several regattas that summer, winning his class at the West Cliff Regatta in August. After one regatta, held at Margate, the weather turned nasty, preventing him from sailing *Spindrift* back to Herne Bay. As he had to get back to his flying, and as Margate Harbour was not the best location to keep a boat for any length of time, Gleed was in something of a dilemma as to what to do for the best. Help, however, came in the shape of a fourteen year-old youngster, himself a keen sailor, by the name of Edward 'Teddy' Denman. This youngster offered to look after the boat for the two weeks before its owner would be able to get away from his flying duties. Look after it he did, even sailing it round to a safer haven at Broadstairs when the weather improved. When Gleed returned a fortnight later he thanked the youngster and then together they sailed *Spindrift* back to Herne Bay.

This was to be the start of a friendship between the two amateur sailors and despite the seven years' age gap, Gleed and Teddy Denman got on well together, Gleed giving him much of his time. Indeed he became his 'crew' and for the remaining months of peace they always sailed together when Gleed was free to do so. When Gleed completed his flying training and went to an operational squadron, he would often fly down to Manston at weekends (usually twice a month) to spend a day or so at Herne Bay and sail with his young friend. Conveniently, Gleed always tried to fly navigation or cross country exercises in the general area of Manston and was quite often 'forced down' there for some minor repairs, which usually occurred on a Friday! Fortunately the machine was always back in service by the Monday morning. The two friends, meantime, would have sailed or competed in a local regatta, before 'skipper' and 'crew' had to part company, the 'crew' looking after the boat until the next time.

Naturally Gleed's parents and sister took an interest in the sailing and the Club's social activities. In 1938, Mrs Gleed presented a bowl to the Herne Bay Sailing Club, called the 'Masters Challenge Bowl', named in memory of her mother (Masters had been Gleed's mother's maiden name). By this time *Spindrift* was firmly established as the Club's fastest 14 foot dinghy, but it was still a thrill to be the first winner of his mother's bowl that June. The next year he was successful on both days of the Royal Temple Yacht Club Regatta.

In August 1938, Gleed took on a more challenging sailing role. Teddy Denman knew a Mr Morris Peatfield who owned an 18-ton Hillyard schooner. Mr Peatfield wanted to sell the vessel, named the *Moronel* and it was decided that a trip to Ostend on the Belgian coast, might show off its paces to would-be purchasers. Through Teddy, Morris Peatfield loaned the *Moronel* to Gleed and his party for the job of showing her off. Gleed, always the natural leader, was skipper, his crew consisting of young sailing friends – Peter Builders, John Bishop, Joe Yates, Brian Peck and of course Teddy Denman in his capacity of 'owner's representative'.

They sailed from Ramsgate Harbour after a gale had almost blown itself out but with a stiff breeze still blowing. Helped by this breeze they logged a speed of 9 knots, as they navigated across the Channel. In Gleed's own words:

> Having at one time thought we were 25 miles from our track, we discovered Ostend under the bowsprit, ... having decided [our] cross bearing compasses b. useless. At last the Royal Yacht Club d'Ostend, where we were welcomed with wizard hospitality.

They had taken just 8½ hours for the crossing and the weather had turned warm and sunny. They docked in Ostend Harbour, and being such a lovely day they decided to go along to the beaches at La Panne to do a little sand yachting. However, the stormy weather which had been over England reached the Belgian coast and the strong winds eventually turned the sand yachts over, one yacht having two of its wheels broken. It then rained and they returned to the *Moronel* extremely damp! When they returned the next day they had a 'lonely slow trip home, 26 hours, light airs and everything set all the way.'

In the event they did not attract any suitable purchasers but the following year a purchaser was found. It was a young RAF pilot by the name of Flying Officer Ian Gleed! Gleed bought the *Moronel* for around £1200 and spent some delightful days tending and sailing her in company with friends from the Club. Yet the *Spindrift* was not neglected, for Gleed and Teddy Denman continued to sail her at weekends, even after the war began. Soon after the war came, however, the *Moronel* had to be laid up at Conyer Creek. It would have to stay laid up till the war's end at which time Gleed dreamed of restoring her to her former greatness and sailing around the world, especially to the South Seas. It was a dream which died with him.

When Gleed was killed, Teddy Denman found his friend had left the boat to him, but his feelings for it without its true skipper were not the same and so he sold her. Today Teddy Denman, a Director with the Minot Insurance Group, still retains his interest and enthusiasm for sailing; among his close friends with a similar passion is the former Prime Minister, Mr Edward Heath. Teddy Denman has a great deal to remember and thank Ian Gleed for. In addition to the friendship which so easily blossomed between them, it was through Gleed that he met the man who first gave him a job for a trial period, when he left school. Thirty-six years later his trial period continues.

During these last years of peace, Ian Gleed, through his association with various sailing clubs, at regattas and other sporting events, met several interesting people. It was all part of the 'in-scene' of those years. He met several writers, Somerset Maugham, Hector Bolitho and Beverley Nichols. One of the more important sportsmen Gleed met at this time was the well known racing driver Raymond Mays who was the number one driver for the ERA team. He too was a part of the scene of the period and on several occasions Gleed and Denman went to Brooklands racing circuit to watch Mays race. Mays recalls:

> I first met Ian Gleed prior to 1939 through my very great friend Wing Commander H.L.P. Lester who was CO of No 3 Squadron at Kenley in Surrey, where Ian Gleed was posted. Knowing that Ian Gleed was interested in motor sport Wing Commander Lester introduced him to me, and we became good friends, and he came over to see me on many occasions, and likewise I visited him at various aerodromes where he was stationed, such as Sutton Bridge, and Digby ...
>
> I may add that I have the happiest memories of Ian as an extremely sincere and good friend, and needless to say, a fabulous pilot.

Raymond Mays introduced Gleed to Beverley Nichols at Brooklands in 1938 when he was writing for the newspapers and had also gone to see Mays race.

Many years later, Nichols, when recalling some of the fighter pilots he had known during World War Two, said that in some he could see what he described as 'VC's eyes'. Of Gleed he recorded:

> Shortly before the war I met a young student whose name was Ian Gleed. He was a nice little chap in a blue blazer, very quiet and polite, and the only reason he appeared was because he had been called downstairs to make a fourth for bridge which he played atrociously. When the game was over my host said: 'What do you think of him?'

I said, 'He's got VC's eyes.'

And he had. They were an exceptionally clear grey and very keen, but there was more to them than that. They seemed to be scanning far horizons.

In 1938 a doctor friend of the Gleeds retired to the south of France and Ian was fortunate in being able to spend a short holiday with him and sail the doctor's boat. It was through this that Gleed met W. Somerset Maugham who also had a villa in the south of France. Maugham invited Gleed to stay at his villa and loaned him his yacht which Ian eagerly sailed on the blue Mediterranean. It was due to his association with Maugham, Bolitho, who lived near to Debden when Gleed was stationed there, and Nichols, that Gleed first thought of writing. When in fact Gleed wrote and published a book in 1942 it was due in part to their influence upon him. The subject of his book came up in conversation between Gleed's old school prefect Ronnie Gethen of Epsom days and another old Epsom boy. The latter, no doubt recalling the Gleed he remembered, was quick to remark that it was news to him that Gleed could even write.

Be that as it may, he could write, he could explore, he was also a fair artist, he could sail – and he could fly.

CHAPTER FOUR

The Pilot

Ever since his son was small, Gleed senior had hoped that Ian would follow him into the medical profession, but like so many sons he had very different ideas about his future. In the event it was Doctor Gleed's daughter Daphne who took the medical field as a career.

As early as fifteen, Ian Gleed had decided that his future was in the skies. He wanted to be a pilot. This desire grew stronger during his last years at Epsom, so strong that he sent off for all the leaflets about a short service commission during his last year. He found that due to his poor academic showing at Epsom that he was unable to apply for a direct entry or as a Cranwell cadet, but probably he would not have liked to join in this way, preferring a short service commission. However, he still needed certain qualifications, so after leaving Epsom, he went to Davis Lang and Dick, the famous crammers in London, to cram for his entrance examinations.

This was typical of Gleed. He rarely did things because he had to or because it was expected, but once he had set his sights on something he really wanted nothing would be allowed to get in his way. Thus, after muddling through school as an indifferent pupil he then spent some months cramming for qualifications that he could, presumably, have gained with ease had he taken the time while at school.

He had already tasted the delights of flying. During one school holiday he had gone to the flying field at Hatfield and enjoyed a 'flip' with the London Aeroplane Club. Before being accepted into the RAF he joined the flying club at Hatfield to try for his civil flying licence.

Over the first few weeks he took his first faltering steps to the skies, starting with dual control, gaining experience and confidence with each flight. Then came his first solo. With that hurdle over he continued with more dual plus the occasional solo, flying Tiger Moths and Gipsy Moth aeroplanes until early 1936 when he received notification of his acceptance for a short service commission. The official date of this acceptance and his SSC was 9 March 1936.

At this time the RAF was rapidly expanding following years of reduced strength since the end of the First World War. During 1936, to help with the expansion plans, a new training system was introduced. Hitherto, the would-be aviators spent a year at an RAF Flying Training School (FTS), after which they undertook further training when they received a posting to an operational squadron. The new system, however, trained the pilot to a stage beyond the twelve months at FTS, so that pilots could take their place in Service squadrons immediately they joined them and then continue in the combined training work of their squadron. This new system began for two main reasons. Firstly it was to enable operational units to concentrate on combined pilot training rather than further semi-basic training of individual flyers, and secondly to meet the demand for a higher output in pure manpower.

The training involved a higher initial standard than that required prior to 1936 and included both day and night flying, navigation and weapon training. In addition the pupil underwent a month's range work at an armament training station. The pupil's training period was divided into three principal stages. First the basic flying stage which involved a civil flying school, operated on a commercial basis whereby the school held an Air Ministry contract. The pupil came under strict discipline, although he lived in civilian conditions and did not wear an RAF uniform. He was taught to handle an aeroplane, was instructed in elementary instrument flying, then progressed to simple cross-country flights. This course of instruction would last approximately eight weeks in summer weather, ten in winter, then the pupil would go to an RAF depot for drill and ground discipline – the inevitable 'square-bashing' – for two weeks.

Following these delights he went to a Service training school for thirteen months,* to progress to service types, take advanced instrument flying instruction, including 'blind' navigation training,

---

*The course was fifteen months if two winter periods were covered.

then progress to fly quite long cross country flights. In addition he would have a good deal of ground instruction work to get through and pass several stiff examinations. If he reached this far he would receive his flying badge and have the dubious honour of being able to carry passengers! (If any could be found to chance it!)

With the fledgling's head firmly in the clouds, he would be posted to an Advanced Flying Training School (AFTS) for a thirteen-week course, fifteen in winter, and as the name implies, the young pilot would continue with all he had been taught but at an advanced level.

Gleed went to a civilian FTS at Filton, near Bristol, in March 1936. There were twenty-three civil flying schools up and down the country which later became known as Elementary and Reserve Flying Training Schools (E & R FTS). Again he flew the Tiger Moth aircraft, the light two-seater biplane which had firmly established itself as the RAF's basic trainer in the 1930's. It had a maximum speed of 104 mph at 1,000 feet, could cruise at 90 mph, had an endurance of three hours, with a service ceiling of 14,000 feet. The type was to remain in service with the RAF until 1951 and even today there are Tiger Moths flying with clubs more than forty years since they first appeared in the skies over England.

Gleed continued his flying instruction, gaining his civil flying licence (Number 8003) on 31 July 1936. By this date, however, he had passed through Filton, completed his period of square-bashing at the RAF Depot at Uxbridge and been posted to No 8 Flying Training School at Montrose, in Scotland; it was a dreary place but he was among many new found friends all with a common goal.

He worked hard that summer of 1936, both in the air and in the classroom. He flew map reading exercises to various parts of the country, went through all the flying drills, emergency drills and all the various tests which a pilot must complete to become a competent aviator. He continually received high assessments and it was quite obvious that with his flair he was destined to fly fighter aeroplanes. He progressed onto the Hawker Hart, Audax and Fury and even flew a Gladiator. By December 1936 he was ready to be sent to a squadron, and although he had been flying single seaters it was not certain that he would achieve his aim of flying fighters until the postings were announced, for one did not always get what one wanted.

Finally the postings were received; the effective day was Christmas Day and it proved to be a wonderful Christmas present. Reading the list of names pinned to the notice board, all the eager young fledgling pilots crowded round, then congratulated or in some cases commiserated with each other on either their good or bad fortune. For Gleed it was good fortune: a posting, as expected, to a fighter squadron – Number 46 Squadron, a fighter unit, based at RAF Kenley in Surrey. He was not the only pilot from 8 FTS posted to 46 Squadron; those assigned were:

Acting Pilot Officer Lloyd Gilbert Schwab
Acting Pilot Officer Ian Richard Gleed
Acting Pilot Officer Patrick Geraint Jameson
Acting Pilot Officer George Stewart Woodwark
Acting Pilot Officer M.S. Scott

Forty-Six Squadron was a famous unit which had been originally formed in 1916 and fought with distinction during the Great War. It had flown two famous single-seat fighter aeroplanes in that conflict, initially the Sopwith Pup then later the Sopwith Camel. Disbanded after the war, 46 Squadron, like Gleed, became part of the RAF's expansion plans. It was reformed at Kenley on 3 September 1936 from B Flight of 17 Squadron under Flight Lieutenant M.F. Calder, and equipped with the Gloster Gauntlet fighter.

The Gauntlet was the last of the open-cockpit fighter biplanes to see service with the RAF. Powered by a 645 hp Bristol Mercury engine it had a maximum speed of 230 mph at 16,000 feet. Its armament consisted of two Vickers machine-guns.

Arriving at Kenley, the new pilots met Flight Lieutenant Calder and some of the others who had come from 17 Squadron, Pilot Officers Johnnie T. Webster, H.C. Jones-Bateman and Sergeant Pilots Steel, Rogers and McPherson, plus another NCO recently arrived from No 4 FTS at Abusuier, Sergeant Christopher F. Currant, known to everyone as 'Bunny'. Strangely enough, Bunny Currant would one day be one of his squadron commanders, in 1942 when Gleed commanded a fighter wing.

On 3 January 1937, Squadron Leader P.R. Barwell took command of the squadron, arriving from the Central Flying School to take up his new command. 46 Squadron, however, lost three of its pilots when Webster, Schwab and Jones-Bateman were sent to

Henlow to join 80 Squadron which was in the process of being reformed. Schwab, a Canadian, was to go to the Middle East with 80 Squadron and later transferred to 112 Squadron where he served gallantly. Flying in North Africa, Greece and Crete he won the DFC and later became a wing commander. Johnnie Webster did not stay long with 80 and when war came he was a flight commander with 41 Squadron. He too fought with distinction during 1940 but was killed in action during the Battle of Britain on 5 September 1940.

Squadron Leader Philip Reginald Barwell, known as 'Dickie' to everyone, was a superb squadron commander, being well liked by everyone. Like Gleed he was on the short side, but also like Gleed had that bubbling cheerfulness which endeared him to all those under his command. Under his leadership the new squadron flourished. At the end of March some of 46 were attached to RAF Hawkinge for an affiliation exercise with 2 (Army Co-operation) Squadron which lasted until 9 April.

However, Gleed got off to a bad start on this day, 31 March. It was a Wednesday and coming in to land at this unfamiliar airfield his wheels hit the top of a house at Gibraltar, Paddlesworth, near Hawkinge. The collision damaged a chimney, made a hole in the roof and scattered tiles into the garden below. Gleed was committed to his landing approach and although he suspected, correctly, that his fixed undercarriage was more than a trifle damaged, decided to continue down to land. In fact part of his undercarriage had been torn off but he touched down gingerly some 200 yards from the house on the western side of the aerodrome. There was a crunch and the Gauntlet tipped forward, the propeller splintered and then the machine turned over. Gleed scrambled out of the wreckage unhurt, a wiser man. The incident was reported briefly in the local newspaper, the aeroplane being said to have been damaged. Gleed, however, confirmed to his family that the Gauntlet had been a write-off! It was his first crash and he had walked away from it thus being able to claim it as a 'good landing!' It was to be his only crash when he was in some way responsible, although he may well have humorously thought that the house, which was unoccupied at the time, should not have got in his way!

Ian Gleed was in his element during this period with 46

Squadron. The world was at his feet. He excelled at his chosen profession, had fulfilled his dream of becoming a fighter pilot and had become a member of 'the greatest flying club in the world', as the peacetime Royal Air Force of the 1930's was often called. He lived in an officers' mess, had a batman to take care of his domestic chores, could eat three square meals a day, share some of the most scintillating company to be found and enjoy the comparative freedom of the skies over England. He was able to soar like an eagle, swoop like a hawk and cavort like a swallow. In his off-duty hours he could enjoy all the sports any young man could desire and when away from the squadron he had his sailing at Herne Bay. Perhaps this period of his young life – he would soon be twenty-one years of age – was the happiest.

From 25 to 29 May he attended a parachute course at RAF Manston but then, shortly after the celebrations which came with his twenty-first birthday, occurred a most exciting event. The annual RAF display at Hendon held each June was fast approaching and to Gleed's delight he was chosen as part of 46 Squadron's fly-past display team. Dickie Barwell chose Pilot Officers H.F. Burton, Cooke, Jameson and Gleed, plus Sergeants Steel, McPherson, Lawson and Mackenzie for the team, these pilots flying to RAF Duxford on 23 June in order to practise for the event. All went well and Gleed with his other eight companions took their bow flying low over the upturned faces of the mighty crowd which packed Hendon on the 26th.

During August the squadron took part in the 1937 Air Exercises, then in November 46 Squadron moved from its Surrey home to RAF Digby in Lincolnshire, part of Fighter Command's 12 Group. By this time command of B Flight (Gleed's) had been taken over by Flight Lieutenant Ernest A. McNab, a Canadian with the RCAF on an exchange attachment with the RAF. In 1940 McNab would command the first RCAF squadron and fly with it during the Battle of Britain.

Gleed continued his round of flying and instructional lectures over the following months, always learning, gaining experience in both flying and leadership. He was consistently being assessed as 'above the average' as pilot/navigator and air gunnery, and as a fighter pilot – 'exceptional'. He would retain these high assessments for the whole of his career. He would need all his expertise soon for the world political scene was fast changing the peaceful face of Europe now that Hitler was dominating Germany. Yet in England life continued much as before although those in the services could sense that confrontation with Hitler's Germany was ahead.

During 1938 Gleed flew in the RAF display for Empire Air Day, 28 May, did some night flying in the Gauntlet and flew the new Hawker Hurricane monoplane fighter. This occurred on 19 November, taking L1567 up for thirty minutes, and carrying out three practice landings.

At the time of the Munich Crisis in September 1938 the silver biplanes of 46 Squadron and all the other aircraft of the RAF, were daubed with green and brown camouflage dope giving the machines an ominously warlike look. The world that September held its breath as deeds of shame were carried out in the name of peace although the breathing space it provided was to do much to win Britain's biggest battle two years ahead. Time stood still briefly but it was time that had been won and was then well used.

The danger of Munich passed. The year ended and in January of the last year of peace 46 Squadron took part in Air Exercises in several parts of the country, testing out local defences.

The squadron bade farewell to their faithful Gauntlets during February. In their place came the new and exciting Hawker Hurricane, whose eight .303 machine-guns were a vast improvement over the Gauntlet's two guns. Munich had allowed time for more and more of the new monoplane fighters to be built and together with the Supermarine Spitfire, the Hurricane gradually replaced almost all the old biplanes during the last eighteen months of peace.

Conversion to the Hurricane was quick and reasonably uneventful. The pilots had a great deal more to get used to, however. They had an enclosed cockpit, the undercarriage was not fixed but had to be retracted. The propeller had a pitch setting control but the speed was the main improvement – over 300 miles per hour in level flight. With a ceiling of 35,000 feet and a rate of climb of 20,000 feet in nine minutes they at last had real power. Nostalgia passed but progress, especially with a war looming on the horizon, was more than welcome in 46 Squadron in the shape of the Hawker Hurricane.

Gleed fell in love with the Hurricane from the start and apart from a brief break at the beginning of 1940 he was to fly Hurricanes in squadron service for nearly three years. The squadron began to collect the new machines from Brooklands during February, Gleed ferrying in L1791 on 6 February, before collecting four more over the next few days. Signs of impending war were brought home on 3 March when Barwell sent Gleed in a Hurricane to RAF Church Fenton to study the camouflage on the aerodrome.

In April, Pat Jameson, three and a half years Gleed's senior in age, was promoted to acting flight lieutenant, becoming B Flight commander when McNab left. Jameson took the flight to Usworth where the squadron took part in further air exercises. On 20 May Gleed flew the Hurricane during the 1939 Empire Air Day display.

There seemed little doubt now that war must come and 1939 saw the squadrons of the RAF increasing their air exercises. 46 Squadron, like all the others, seemed continually in the air that summer, flying in local air defence flights or searchlight cooperation duties at Abbotsinch, over the Firth of Forth, the Clyde, Speke and Acklington. Then on 1 September 1939 Germany invaded Poland and the RAF was mobilized for war. By this date Gleed had amassed a useful total of 640 flying hours.

Two days later, Sunday, 3 September, Gleed was woken by his batman at 7.30 am. He could hear some of his pals in their nearby rooms as they too were awoken to begin their usual noisy domestic chores. Less than an hour later, following breakfast, they drove to the squadron hangars in some of the pilots' cars from where they taxied their Hurricanes to the squadron's dispersal points. 46 Squadron came to 'Readiness' by 8.30 am. They remained near the machines all that morning. The pilots were silent, not their usual boisterous selves. They spoke little, each left with his own thoughts of what was to come, the future, their future, now uncertain.

Squadron Leader Barwell arrived at dispersal shortly before 11 o'clock. What's happening, they asked, any news, how long shall we remain at readiness, etc? Barwell knew little more than they did but he believed the situation grave.

'Have you got a wireless out here?' he asked, 'Chamberlain is broadcasting at eleven.'

'I've got my car radio,' offered Gleed, 'what time is it?' It was nearly 11 am and shortly the sound of Big Ben chimed 11 o'clock. In silence they all listened to the Prime Minister, Neville Chamberlain, as he told the world that Britain was once again at war with Germany. The pilots and ground crews too crowded round the car as the fateful words were spoken. So it was war. As professional servicemen they had always known that they might well have to fight at some stage of their careers. They were trained and ready although each one of them fully realised that life as they had known would be very different now. Nothing would ever be the same again.

They sat about or laid out on the grass while the airmen huddled together near the Hurricanes. The sun was warm. At any moment they might have to take-off and fight German aeroplanes. In the meantime, they waited – as it turned out, they had to wait for some time.

That night, as if to remind everyone that war had really been declared, there were two air-raid warnings. A Flight under Flight Lieutenant Stewart, were ordered into the air but no attacks materialised. It was all an anti-climax.

The anti-climax of the war that just didn't happen continued throughout September and into October. Signs of war appeared, however. The station's buildings were camouflaged, tin hats were issued and gas masks had to be carried from place to place. Then in October the squadron was ordered to North Coates, near Hull. They were to be at a state of advanced readiness to protect shipping off and in the Humber. B Flight took off first on 12 October, flew to North Coates and landed, were refuelled and then they sat at cockpit readiness. Later that morning Jameson, Gleed and the others were ordered up to cover a convoy of ships off Spurn Head. They found the ships and were warmly welcomed by exploding anti-aircraft shells as the 'friendly' ship's destroyer escort adopted the safety first attitude of shoot first and ask questions later. Not unnaturally the Hurricane pilots were a little peeved so they kept right away and out of range, covering the convoy from a safe distance for an hour before turning for home. As they reached North Coates again they saw that A Flight had arrived and that already they were taking off to continue the patrol over the ships.

Jameson led his flight into land and it shook the pilots to discover that Sergeant Lawson's Hurricane had a lump of Royal Navy shrapnel in it! At the end of the day the squadron returned to Digby. This daily duty continued during October, each morning the squadron flying to North Coates, and either patrolling or remaining at readiness through the day, then returning home in the evening the squadron was released. Little was seen until the 21st. Jameson and his flight had just been relieved by A Flight led on this occasion by Dickie Barwell, when control radioed to Barwell, warning him that unidentified aircraft were approaching from the east. Gleed, cursing his luck at missing all the fun, heard Barwell acknowledge the message as he and the others continued back to base to refuel quickly in the hope of being sent out again.

Meanwhile, Barwell, leading Red Section of A Flight (in L1802) with Pilot Officer P.J. Frost (L1801), Flight Sergeant E. Shackley (L1817) and Yellow Section, Pilot Officer R.M.J. Cowles (L1815), Pilot Officer R.P. Plummer (L1805), and Pilot Officer P.W. Lefevre (L1892), watched the eastern sky for signs of approaching aircraft.

Barwell received another message from control; 12 enemy aircraft heading in from the southeast at 1,000 feet. The convoy 46 Squadron was protecting this chilly October afternoon was now five miles east of Spurn Head.

'Bandits nine o'clock below,' yelled Barwell as he spotted the German formation which he recognised as a dozen Heinkel He115 torpedo-carrying floatplanes. Barwell led the attack, selecting the left hand aeroplane which he lined up in his sights and fired into from 400 yards. Flames shot out from the Heinkel's starboard engine and the aeroplane fell away towards the sea but as the enemy pilot tried to level out above the water the starboard wing of his aircraft, now burning fiercely, folded back and the Heinkel crashed. Pilot Officer Frost also hammered at a Heinkel and this too burst into flames and crashed.

Barwell pulled up and round, attacking another Heinkel, damaging it and it was then attacked by Cowles and Shackley and then Plummer. As Plummer closed in, Barwell ordered him to get in closer before firing, which he did, and after his attack the Heinkel tipped forward and hit the sea, sending up a huge water fountain. Frost and Lefevre chased a fourth Heinkel, each taking turns to fire at it until, with both engines stopped, it landed on the water. Four for no loss was a great success in this the squadron's first engagement of the war. Return fire had put a few bullets into a couple of the Hurricanes but otherwise the squadron suffered no injuries. Jameson and Gleed were happy for Barwell and the squadron, but still disappointed that the Germans hadn't shown up before their patrol time had come to an end. That night, back at Digby, they had a terrific thrash in the mess to celebrate 46's first victories of World War Two.

RAF Digby was graced with a visit by His Majesty King George VI on 2 November; Dickie Barwell introduced all his pilots to the King as he made his inspection. The pilots, standing in flying clothes and wearing their 'Mae Wests' stood to attention in front of their Hurricanes as the King spoke briefly to each of them. For Ian Gleed it was the first time he had spoken to his King – but it was not to be the last.

CHAPTER FIVE
Flight Commander

Five days after the King's visit, Dickie Barwell invited Gleed to his
house for a drink, which, as it was a lone invitation, he thought a
little unusual. When he arrived Barwell gave him the news.

'You have been posted as flight commander to ~~226~~ Squadron
which has recently formed at Sutton Bridge.' 266

Gleed was tremendously pleased and excited although sorry to
leave the squadron which had been his home for nearly three years.
Yet this was promotion and a chance to command a flight which
could only be good. As it turned out Barwell himself was posted to
Sutton Bridge as station commander and he also received the DFC
at the end of November for his part in the attack on the Heinkels.
All this was just cause to have yet another party which as always
carried on far into the night.

Gleed was sad at leaving, for he left many friends and comrades
with whom he had trained and flown with for so long. His flight
commander, Pat Jameson, went on to achieve great things as a
fighter pilot and wing leader. After an adventure in Norway,
Jameson later led the Wittering and West Malling wings, and by
November 1943 was a group captain. In the following year he
commanded a Tempest Wing, having by that time received the
DSO, DFC and bar.

Dickie Barwell later commanded RAF Station Biggin Hill,
perhaps the most famous fighter station of the war. As station
commander and a group captain he was not supposed to fly on
operations but this did not stop him. On one occasion taking off to
accompany the Biggin Hill Wing on a sweep his engine cut out and
he was forced to crash-land in the valley to the west of Biggin. The
Spitfire was written-off and Barwell finished up with a broken
vertebra. Yet within two weeks, encased in plaster, he was back on

duty and flying again, usually as number two to Wing Commander R. Duke-Wooley DFC, Biggin Hill's wing leader. It was a sad day when in July 1942 Barwell took-off in a Spitfire VI to intercept a high flying German reconnaissance aeroplane in company with another Spitfire. Unknown to them, two other Spitfires from Tangmere also raced to their Spitfires and took after the German. Although warned by control, Barwell's radio must have been u/s. The second two Spitfires saw the new, different shape of the Spitfire VI and in one of those tragic incidents that happen in war, Barwell was shot down into the Channel and lost.

Undoubtedly Gleed's sadness at leaving 46 was heightened the following May when 46 Squadron, including some of the pilots with whom he had flown, were practically wiped out when the aircraft carrier HMS *Glorious* was sunk off Norway. Led by its new CO, Squadron Leader K.B.B. Cross, 46 went to Norway and were based at Bardufoss. Eleven days after their arrival, 8 June 1940, they were forced to evacuate and it became necessary to destroy all their Hurricanes. However, in a gallant attempt to save the aeroplanes, the remaining pilots, with sandbags weighting the tails of the Hurricanes, successfully landed on *Glorious*. This success was short lived when the carrier ran into the enemy battleships *Scharnhorst* and *Gneisenau* who quickly sank *Glorious* with their big guns. Only Cross and Pat Jameson survived; the other pilots including Flight Lieutenant Stewart, Flying Officers Robert Cowles and Philip Frost and Flight Sergeant Shackley who had been so successful in 46 Squadron's first combat, were all lost together with the machines they had tried to save. Gleed's own Hurricane L1804, in which he had flown regularly during 1939 was lost in this expedition, as was L1815 and L1892 which had also seen action on 21 October.

RAF Sutton Bridge, where Gleed was posted as flight commander of 266 Squadron, was more familiarly known to pre-war fighter pilots as an armament camp. Here they would attend an annual air gunnery course, which usually lasted two to three weeks.

No 266 Squadron had only been reformed on 30 October and it was still very much in its embryo state when Flight Lieutenant (Acting) Gleed arrived. Its commanding officer was Squadron Leader J.W.A. Hunnard who at nearly thirty-three years of age was quite 'old' when compared with the ages of his young pilots. He was in consequence soon known as 'Daddy' by them all. Gleed was put in command of B Flight, while A Flight was commanded by Flight Lieutenant J.B. Coward.

James Coward, a year or so Gleed's senior, recalls the first time he and Gleed reported to their new commander: 'He told us that he would expect a lot of help from Gleed and me, as he had only been a flight lieutenant eight years. We were both highly amused as we had also got temporary rank after only about one year as flying officers.'

Coward also recalls:

The squadron was initially equipped with Miles Magisters, which we began flying on 11 November as no Spitfires were then available and in any case the remaining pilots were all, as far as I can remember, trained on Ansons at FTS for Bomber Command. On 4 December we collected out first Fairey Battles, which we flew until 19 January 1940 when Ian flew me over to Brize Norton to collect the first of our Spitfires – N3118.

Gleed did indeed fly Coward to Brize Norton in a Fairey Battle, L5375, Coward sitting in the rear seat. While his brother flight commander brought back one machine, Gleed flew back a second one – N3175. He repeated the exercise the next day but this time took Pilot Officer Hancock in a Battle, then flew back N3120.

During those first months with the squadron all three senior pilots were kept very busy working up the squadron and the severe winter weather did little to assist them. Several Fairey Battle light single-engined bombers were in 266 Squadron at this time although Gleed also flew a Bristol Blenheim a few times, his first twin-engined machine. The first Battles were collected from No 24 MU – Maintenance Unit – on 4 December, and as already mentioned the first Spitfires collected from 6 MU at Brize Norton on 19 January.

Ian Gleed felt the difference between the Hurricane and Spitfire straight away. That extra kick in the back when the Spitfire accelerated along the runway. One wing down slightly, caused by the torque of the airscrew as he left the ground, the sensitivity of the controls and the extra speed once in the air. He could hardly wait to have a go at the enemy although at this moment little had really happened in this, the period known as the 'phoney war'.

The first air battles had been fought over Scotland when German aircraft made occasional bombing attacks on units of the Royal Navy in the Firth of Forth, and other air actions had taken place over France. There were four Hurricanes squadrons in France, No's 1, 73, 85 and 87. 1 and 73 saw more action than the other two but mostly it was just reconnaissance aeroplanes that they engaged. Gleed had little idea at the beginning of 1940 that it would still be some months before he saw action, or that it would not be in a Spitfire and that it would in fact be in France that he would first fire his guns in anger at his country's enemies.

Before these events were to occur, he was to experience his second crash, or to be accurate, he would actually depart from a crippled aeroplane. This happened on the afternoon of 18 February 1940. The pressures on Coward and Gleed to get their flights operational were immense, but almost all the pilots had now converted onto the Spitfires. By the 18th only two pilots had still to fly their first Spitfire solo flights and these in fact were flown satisfactorily early that afternoon.

No sooner were these two machines down than Gleed decided to test fly a new Spitfire which so far had only been flown on short hops at low altitude. It was one of Gleed's tasks to test all his flight's Spitfires at a rated height, in this case 18,000 feet.

The afternoon was cold and a cruel wind blew across the airfield. Snow still lay thick on the ground and clouds skudded overhead at around 5,000 feet.

Taking Spitfire N3120 up into the wintry sky he climbed quickly, putting the machine through its paces by climbing flat out. Looking down he could see the whole of the Wash, noticing casually that the tide was out. He saw the sandbanks showing and the sailor in him guessed it would be a difficult place in which to sail his boats. Seconds later he entered the clouds but still climbing hard finally shot out into a brilliant sunlit sky. As he climbed in large circles the clouds below looked beautiful in the warm sunshine. Above was a further cloud layer but through large gaps in it he could see a huge expanse of blue.

He levelled out at 18,000 feet and proceeded to check the Spitfire's instruments. To his experienced eye all seemed well and he opened the throttle fully, the rev counter resting on 2850. The only fault he could find was that the machine seemed to be flying a trifle right wing low. Time to go home. Easing back on the throttle he nosed down into a gentle dive. The speed rose as he began a slight left hand turn, and he closed the radiator. Then there was a sudden crack!

He was shot forward violently, his safety harness cutting into his shoulders. He tried to lift his head but was completely unable to do so. Then there was a bang and he passed out. What exactly happened is obscure. Whether the Spitfire just broke up, iced up or as Gleed's school chum Reg Medlock recalled Ian telling him, the leading edge of one wing opened up, is not clear. Whatever did occur so suddenly, the rapid deceleration − or just the act of the Spitfire breaking up − shot Ian Gleed right through the perspex cockpit canopy which, not unnaturally, rendered him unconscious. How long he remained unconscious will also never be known, but he came to with his muddled mind slowly registering, firstly that he was no longer in the aeroplane, secondly that he was not dead and lastly, that although apparently out of the cockpit he felt no sensation of falling. Almost as a reflex action having finally decided in those few brief seconds of semi-consciousness, that he must be hurtling towards the earth below, he felt for his parachute's D-ring, pulled it, at the same moment realising that he could not see. As the parachute opened above him he passed out once again.

When he came round for the second time he was bumping along the ground; the strong wind dragging him and the billowing parachute canopy along the rough surface of a field. Again his reflexes automated his arm and hand and he thumped the parachute's quick release box situated on his lower chest. The harness fell away and he stopped bumping over the ground and lay still. He still could not see and thought that he must be blind. Also his left arm and right leg were causing him excruciating pain. He felt the snow about him, and as his right foot felt cold and wet gathered he had lost his right shoe. He began to shiver in the cold. If he didn't move he would freeze to death, he thought, but as he tried to move so the pain in his arm and leg stopped him. He pulled off his flying helmet and his head and hair felt sticky − blood, he correctly assumed. As the cold began to cut through him he tried again to move, actually managing to crawl a short distance by using his right arm and keeping his left one firmly against his side. Then he heard voices and knew he had been found. In a strong Lincolnshire accent he heard someone say:

'Gawd, doesn't 'e look a bluedy mess?'

Gleed agreed with the voice that he was a mess and that he felt equally awful. The voices asked if he had been alone in the aeroplane to which he confirmed he had been. He asked where the Spitfire was.

'It be orl in pieces,' replied another voice.

He was still very cold and asked for a coat or blanket to be placed over him and a moment later felt something being put over his body which immediately reduced the biting effect of the wind and made him feel a little better. Then a car arrived and someone said that a doctor was on his way. Gradually, as he lay quietly, the darkness turned to grey, pink, then a little by little he began to see. Actually what had happened was that the blood had poured from his head wound, covered his eyes and forehead, then congealed during his descent. The light snow that had been falling as he lay on the ground, together with the damp air, had gradually softened the caked blood allowing him to open his eyes. He gave thanks as his sight returned.

He lifted his head and saw the three men who had come to his aid. Nearby stood an Austin Ten car and he saw he had been covered by a coat and some sacking. He asked his helpers to get him into the car which they did. His leg gave him a lot of pain and his head felt as if it might fall off at any moment but he found if he did not move his arm it didn't hurt. They drove him slowly to a nearby farm house where he gratefully accepted a cup of coffee from a lady. Not long afterwards an RAF ambulance and doctor arrived and a needle was jabbed into his arm.

Although dimly aware of his arrival at the hospital he finally passed out. He awoke some time later flat on his back, his arm in plaster and his head and leg swathed in bandages. A nurse was sitting by his bed and leaning over him said reassuringly:

'You're all right, laddie.'

He had come down at Little Ouse near Littleport, the Spitfire having crashed nearby at 2.40 pm. He had been taken to Littleport hospital. A doctor arrived at the hospital later that day and casually ran his eye down the list of names which constituted the day's arrival of patients. His eye stopped at Flight Lieutenant I.R.

Gleed RAF. Entering the ward he asked the sister to show him the bed in which the RAF man lay, and went over and introduced himself.

'Are you any relation to Doctor Seymour Gleed of Finchley?' Gleed confirmed that he was his son. 'I used to be on the staff of the Finchley Memorial Hospital so I know your father quite well. Is there anything I can do for you?'

'Yes, please. Could you telephone my parents to say that I'm all right? And I seem to have lost my wristwatch!'

As good as his word the doctor telephoned the Gleed household that Sunday afternoon and later Gleed himself sent a telegram to his family which read:

Have had slight accident, address will be RAF Littleport, Ely, Cambs, stop. Don't worry. Ian.

Not long afterwards his watch was returned to him. It had been found near where he had landed and was quickly handed in at the hospital. He remained in the hospital for some weeks then went to the RAF convalescent hospital at Torquay. After much badgering he was finally allowed to go before a medical board, who, to his utter disgust, allowed him to return to his unit but only allowed him to fly dual until a further board in three weeks' time. To Gleed this seemed completely absurd as his unit was a single-seat fighter squadron! His next board, this time at RAF Uxbridge, also passed him fit to return to the squadron but still not to fly single seaters. Almost immediately he took himself off on leave with a ten day pass in his pocket. He motored down to Herne Bay and the sea.

With his leave over he returned to RAF Martlesham, where 266 Squadron had since moved but, although he was greeted warmly, he found that in the interim another flight commander had taken over his command. He understood the situation and equally Squadron Leader Hunnard could do nothing about it. However, he took a dual flying test on 23 April, with Flight Lieutenant Cooke taking him up in a Miles Magister (P2458). He was then allowed to fly Magisters during the rest of April and early May. His last flight with 266 was flown on 10 May.

On this date, the balloon went up in France. The Germans had finally ended the 'phoney war' by their sudden attacks into Holland and Belgium. The war was suddenly very real. A Hurricane squadron at Martlesham took off with a flourish to fly a patrol over the Hook of Holland, while the pilots of 266 watched enviously. They awaited their return with more than a little interest and finally the Hurricanes came straggling back – those that did get back! Seven landed which meant five had been lost. They had, the others quickly learned, run into a large number of German fighters and the pilots to whom Gleed spoke seemed visibly shaken by their experience. Their CO and one of the flight commanders were among the missing.

Gleed was frustrated at being on the ground and equally annoyed that he had yet to be passed fit for normal flying duties. Without a clean bill of health, a flight, or a real purpose now that the war had really started, he was soon getting on even his own CO's nerves as he wandered aimlessly about. Finally on 14 May, a postagram slip arrived which with some relief Hunnard read to him:

Flight Lieutenant Gleed posted to 87 Squadron, BEF, France. To proceed to RAF Halton on receipt of signal for Medical Board. Report to Uxbridge following day if fit for full flying duties – signed – Air Ministry.

Gleed was over the moon and rushing about like a man in torment to get packed and away. With his car bursting at the seams he roared off in the general direction of Halton, cursing the lack of signposts in a wartime, security conscious England, but finally arrived at his destination. After a hurried lunch he found his way to the medical buildings where for the next hour or so he was prodded and probed, then left waiting for the final verdict. Two men ahead of him were told they had failed and would not be able to fly again which gave Gleed a few anxious moments, in which to pray fervently for a pass.

His prayers were answered and within minutes he was on the telephone to Hunnard who promised to fix everything up, leaving his ex-flight commander to arrive at Uxbridge the next morning.

He motored home to Finchley for one last night with his mother, father and sister, knowing, all knowing, that the next day he would be off to France and the war. His total of flying hours by this time was 737.

Of all the things Gleed had gained or acquired during his first years with the Royal Air Force, the one which stayed with him until his death was his nickname. Nicknames are quickly earned or given in any group of men and the Royal Air Force was no exception. Gleed's nickname became 'Widge' or sometimes 'The Widge'. While it is not completely certain who gave him this term or indeed how exactly it was derived, it seemed certain that it was a reference to both his size and his favourite word. Most things to Gleed were 'wizard' and because of his small stature he was at first referred to as the 'Wizard Midget' which in turn was shortened to 'Widge'. It was a term of affection and not in any way derisory, and he took the term with him into history.

CHAPTER SIX

To the war

Eighty-Seven Squadron had flown to France as part of the Air Component on 9 September 1939, just six days following the declaration of war. With its sister squadron, Number 85, these two units comprised the two fighter squadrons in 60 Wing, commanded by Wing Commander J.A. Borét MC AFC.

From September 1939 until 10 May 1940, 87 Squadron flew patrols, practised, scrambled after elusive German reconnaissance aeroplanes, practised, flew escort missions and – practised some more. It had only occasional successes in combat. Flight Lieutenant R. Voase-Jeff shot down the squadron's first enemy aircraft of World War Two on 2 November 1939, destroying a Heinkel He111, which was also the first Heinkel bomber to fall to the Royal Air Force in France. For this action the French Government awarded him the French Croix de Guerre. Pilot Officer W.D. David severely damaged a second Heinkel in the same action. It was not until 11 April of the following year that the squadron's second confirmed victory came. On this occasion Pilot Officer Johnnie Cock shot down another Heinkel.

Unlike the two Hurricane squadrons, 1 and 73, of the Advanced Air Striking Force, 87 and 85 did not see the number of pre-blitz combats that they did, but when the German attacks on the Western Front commenced on 10 May all four squadrons were equally engaged as well as other squadrons which were sent to France following the beginning of the Blitzkreig. Although most of 87 Squadron's records were lost in France when they had to finally retreat, history does record that it gave a good account of itself during the ten days 10 to 20 May 1940. Like the other Hurricane squadrons, not forgetting the RAF's light bombers, the Blenheims and Battles, the fighter pilots of 87 Squadron were in the thick of the battle from the first day. Many feats of heroism occurred during that period, many of which will never be known because many of the pilots who made them died fighting against great odds. Commanded by Squadron Leader J.S. 'Johnnie' Dewar, 87 Squadron shot down at least thirteen German aircraft on the first day, six more on the 11th, and a further five on the 12th. By the 17th it had accounted for over forty German aircraft but had suffered severe losses too. The squadron stars had begun to emerge. Bobby Voase-Jeff, Denis David, Roland Beamont, Roddy Rayner, Harry Mitchell, Chris Darwin, Gareth Nowell as well as Johnnie Dewar.

When Ian Gleed received his posting to 87 on 14 May, Flying Officer Jack Campbell, acting flight commander, had just been killed. 87's A Flight needed a leader – Gleed was available. He arrived on the 17th, exactly one week after the German invasion of France and the Netherlands. Although an experienced pilot, he had not seen any combat. Even so he was posted right into the front line at a moment when the shooting war was in full swing.

Saying goodbye to his mother, father and sister Daphne, Gleed drove to RAF Uxbridge where he was immediately put in charge of a party of three hundred airmen who were also going to France. Assisted by another pilot he and his party proceeded to the south coast by troop train, boarded a troopship and sailed to France that evening. His thoughts as he crossed the English Channel were for his family. They had always been very close and their thoughts too were for him. He was mindful that during the First War, a pilot's life on the Western Front was, on average, measured in weeks. He was now on his way to the new Western Front, to fly and fight over the same areas which the flyers of that war had flown and fought. Another question which exercised his mind that evening was what was the average life expectancy in this war. He was soon to discover that the average was no better than that of the dark days of 1916- 17; in fact during those ten days in May 1940 it was worse.

From the French port of entry, Gleed travelled by train which he found more comfortable than the earlier troop train, for he and his companion were even served with a chicken and champagne dinner. As the evening grew dark he was rather surprised at the apparent slackness of the French black-out. Arriving at Lille, he found an air-raid in progress. Anti-aircraft guns were firing while searchlights probed the dark sky above. There was a distant sound of exploding bombs and the dull roar of aero engines which seemed to herald his arrival at the war.

The railway station was packed with refugees and all the lights had been switched off for the duration of the raid. Gleed managed to find a telephone and got through to the squadron's base; the adjutant suggested that he remain in Lille for the night at the Metropole Hotel. The adjutant promised to have him collected the next morning, the 17th. Gleed reluctantly agreed although he thought it strange to have to wait at a place that was being bombed when in all probability the airfield was at that moment free from attack. He eventually found the hotel in the darkness only to discover that it was full, although the bar was occupied in part by Hurricane pilots of 504 Squadron. After several drinks with them he and another pilot drifted off to another hotel but were only allowed to stay if they agreed to share a room which cost them 50 francs.

The next morning Gleed was collected and driven out of the town to Seclin airfield, being dropped at what he later described as a cricket pavilion. Outside, in the morning sunshine, lounged several pilots on deck chairs. The first pilot he met was Pilot Officer R.F. 'Watty' Watson who was busily engaged in building a model aeroplane. Over the next year he would come to know Watty very well and learn to live with and accept his absorbing hobby of making and flying model aeroplanes. Gleed was introduced to the other pilots and later met the CO, Johnnie Dewar. 87 Squadron was more than pleased to have him; he was certainly needed. Roland Beamont recalls Gleed's arrival:

Gleed was one of our replacement pilots and he came out from the UK to tell us exactly how to run the war – all 5ft 6ins of him! He was immediately as good as his word and tore into the enemy on every conceivable occasion with apparent delight and entire lack of concern. His spirit was exactly what was needed to bolster up the somewhat stunned survivors of the week following 10 May. That is not to say that 87 Squadron's morale was not extremely high, but The Widge somehow managed to raise it further.

In comparison with the previous week, the 17th was a little quieter, although patrols were flown and Roddy Rayner shot down a Messerschmitt 110; Watty Watson damaged another. Gleed took the time to sort himself out a new aeroplane, and was assigned P2798, a Hawker Hurricane which he collected that same day. He and Watson flew to the local aeroplane depot and picked up two new Hurricanes. Gleed took P2798, Watson P2829. Back at Seclin Gleed's machine was marked with the squadron code letters LK and individual aircraft letter A, while Watson's was marked LK-G. Both of these Hurricanes were to be the longest serving aeroplanes in 87, surviving to the autumn of 1941, a very long time for any aeroplane to survive, especially during such an action filled period of air operations. During one sortie over France a single bullet passed right through a wing of Watson's Hurricane and for some reason it was never patched or repaired. Finally it became a sort of 'badge of courage' and remained visible right up till the end of its days. On the side of his cockpit Gleed had painted the Walt Disney cat 'Figaro' from Pinocchio. He could have no idea then that he and Figaro – P2798 – would be together for a long time.

Gleed and others of A and B Flights were woken at 3.30 am the following morning and called to Readiness. After a hurried breakfast they clambered aboard their Citroen van and trundled off in the pre-dawn to the squadron's dispersal areas. The sun slowly rose into a cloudless blue sky, heralding Ian Gleed's first day on operations in France. The squadron was scheduled to fly two sections, one each from A and B Flights, on a dawn patrol across the front lines towards the Belgian border, then fly towards the capital Brussels. They were also required to patrol to the River Oise and keep an eye open for any signs of enemy tank movements in that area. In the air they were due to rendezvous with two sections from 85 Squadron over Lille. Take off was at six o'clock. At 5.50 am the Hurricane's engines burst into life and Gleed climbed into the cockpit of P2798 for their first war operation together. From across the aerodrome Gleed saw the section of B Flight about to take off as he and his section moved forward, then gained speed to roar over the grass field, then lift into the morning air.

The six Hurricanes met up with 85 Squadron but there was only one section making a total of only nine Hurricanes. Together they all climbed to 12,000 feet. Flying away from Lille they began to experience sporadic anti-aircraft fire. Gleed and the others began to weave gently from side to side and change height but the black explosions followed them. However nobody was hit and a short time later the firing ceased. They flew on peacefully, the haze of Brussels could be clearly seen on the horizon and soon they could make out the church steeples and high buildings of the city. As Gleed searched for the first time a hostile sky his eyes suddenly spotted the enemy. Five tiny specks below making their way towards them. Gleed waggled his wings and flicked on his R/T switch.

'Bandits one o'clock below; line astern, Go!'

His section, Watson and Chris Darwin, followed him as he

France 1940

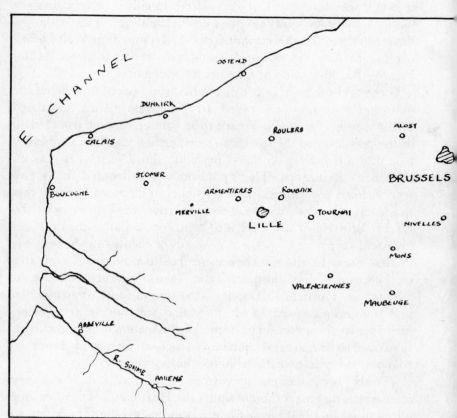

stayed on course, then turned gently to get into the best position to attack. It was hot in the cockpit, the sun beating down from the still cloudless sky. Keeping the enemy in sight Gleed and the others searched the expanse of sky in case other Germans were about; each man peered through gloved fingers into the rays of the sun but nothing else was in sight.

'Let's go,' said Gleed and he gently pushed forward on the stick, Watson and Darwin doing the same as they went into a gentle dive to gain speed, then hauling back went into a right hand bank; they dropped down into a diving turn as the enemy aircraft, which they could now identify as twin-engined Messerschmitt 110 fighters, sailed serenely on underneath them, flying in a wide vic formation. Swooping down, Gleed selected the right-hand German, ordering his section into 'Echelon port, Go!'

The Germans had not seen them, being completely oblivious to the Hurricanes now diving steeply upon them from the sun. Gleed throttled back so as not to overshoot his target but then the 110s broke – they had finally seen the danger. The leading Messerschmitt and his companions turned steeply to meet the six Hurricanes (the three machines of 85 Squadron had not, for some reason, turned with 87). Gleed and the others tried to get in a quick shot as the two formations met but although a 110 fired at him and Gleed saw the lines of tracer bullets reach out for him, he had no chance to fire in return before he roared through the enemy fighters. As the Hurricanes and Messerschmitts flashed by each other, so close Gleed thought they must surely collide, the rear gunners opened fire, and a line of tracer shells streamed over Gleed's cockpit canopy.

Once clear, Gleed pulled P2798 into a steep left hand turn but there were more 110s who seemed to have suddenly appeared from above. Apparently the shimmering blue sky had held more enemy fighters high up who had now come down as the Hurricanes committed themselves. Gleed saw a Hurricane turn over, burst into flames and then saw a parachute open. He turned with two grey-green coloured 110s, their rear gunners firing back at him but he could turn tighter than them and got in a good deflection shot inside the turn. Ignoring the bullets flashing past him Gleed jabbed at the gun button on the circular control column grip. His fire ripped into one of the Messerschmitts' petrol tanks and a second later the whole wing erupted in flames. The 110 turned over onto its back, leaving a trail of smoke and flame as it fell away. Gleed watched in fascination as the enemy aeroplane spiralled down belching smoke and fire until it dived into a wood and blew up.

Still turning, Gleed found himself in the centre of three circling Messerschmitts, each of whose rear gunners were firing at him. One sailed up in front of him, filling his reflector gun sight and he fired at no more than 25 yards range. His Hurricane shook from the recoil of his eight guns – then blackness. Oil sprayed over his windscreen but as he pulled up and round he looked back and down, seeing the 110 fall away and explode as it too hit the ground. His oil smeared windscreen cleared sufficiently for him to see forward again and he went after another 110, pressed his gun button but nothing happened – he was out of ammunition. The sky still seemed full of Messerschmitts and with empty guns he decided to leave while able to do so. Stick over and back, he half rolled and dived clear, then, levelling out, hedge-hopped towards Lille and home. Off to one side he found another Hurricane also flying home low but it had been shot-up and the pilot was struggling to keep the machine in the air. Just as Gleed formated on it, it dipped towards the ground and crashed into the side of a house.

The after-battle reaction now set in. Gleed was sweating and shaking. Looking at his wristwatch he was amazed to discover that it was only six-thirty am. Utterly lost he flew north knowing that eventually he must reach the Channel coast where he could make his way to Seclin once he had orientated himself. He silently cursed the squadron's lack of English maps (they only had French ones) and his own sparse knowledge of the French countryside, although this was hardly surprising. He had been in France scarcely 36 hours. As the sea came into view some minutes later he spotted an aerodrome right on the coast and coming in to land he saw French markings on the aeroplanes standing by the runway. As he landed and gunned his engine to taxi in, French airmen ran to meet him. He cut the engine, jumped down but failed to understand a single word the Frenchmen were saying but then a *Capitaine*, using a smattering of broken schoolboy English, informed him that he had landed at Berck-sur-Mer near Le Touquet.

They drove him to their château mess where he was given coffee. His hands were still shaking, so much so that he could not stop the cup rattling against the saucer. He then gratefully ate a hearty breakfast. He was still shaking but managed to explain to his hosts that he had just shot down two Messerschmitts which seemed to please them. Later, with the gift of another map and directions from the *Capitaine*, Gleed, his Hurricane refuelled, took off again to return safely to Seclin. To his relief Watson and Darwin were both back unhurt. Watty had also destroyed a 110 and Darwin claimed one 'probably destroyed'. They both thought that their new flight commander had been lost and were wondering who would take over the flight. They then climbed back into the Citroen and drove off to their mess for breakfast, for Gleed his second breakfast of the morning.

The rest of the morning remained quiet but after lunch Johnnie Dewar led a patrol of squadron strength over Brussels. They saw some Me109s and Gleed's section gave chase, but they flew off so the Hurricanes broke off and left them to it. That evening the wing escorted Blenheims to Namur, anti-aircraft fire bringing down one Hurricane but the pilot baled out. Later Me109s dived on the British formation, two Hurricanes being hit and falling in flames. Then the bombs went down, and then the formation was heading for home. It had been a busy day. Three sorties and two kills on his first day was, more than a creditable start, but the German advance was still pressing forward. The Allied armies were being pushed back almost continually at every point along the front.

The next morning, 19 May, Gleed and the others were at Readiness by 6.30 am. It was another warm morning giving promise of another hot day. The road which ran near the aerodrome was becoming crammed with the pitiful sight of refugees, some with cars, others with horse and carts, bicycles, prams, or just walking with their few possessions upon their backs or in their arms. According to some of them the Germans were only some thirty kilometres away. The line of people was heading slowly westwards and stories of strafing by German aircraft were heard. Families had lost sons, mothers, friends and even the few possessions they had salvaged. Others had become separated, taken wrong turnings or just wandered off in a daze. To the RAF pilots their plight seemed to encourage them to try and do more though they themselves were becoming totally shocked and dazed at the constant action and the air battles in which they always seemed to be vastly outnumbered. The Luftwaffe seemed supreme and no matter how many German aircraft they shot down there still seemed to be more of them the next time.

Johnnie Dewar telephoned operations for orders but confusion was setting in and little was known about the front lines. At 10 am, as the pilots stood at dispersal in the sunshine, two Westland Lysander two-seat army co-operation aircraft flew over and circled the aerodrome, presumably about to land. Then several Messerschmitt 109s swooped down, guns blazing. The Hurricane pilots ran to their machines which the ground crews were starting up. Dismissing with a wave of his hand his ground crew who were wanting to help strap him in, Gleed opened up the throttle. The engine roared and surging forward he raced and bounced across the aerodrome then lifted off, two other Hurricanes close on his heels. He pulled up his undercarriage feeling the spinning wheels bump up underneath him as he opened up the throttle fully. Looking back he saw two columns of smoke rising from a nearby wood where the two Lysanders had gone in, and a parachute hanging in the air.

At full boost he raced after the 109s which he now observed numbered five. They were racing away at full speed but gradually he began to close the gap between them as they reduced speed thinking themselves safe from harm. The 'hit and run' Messerschmitts were oblivious of his presence as he came closer and closer, resisting strongly the urge to open fire too soon. He had to get in close. He was angry but also excited and wanted to hit back at these particular Germans. At 200 yards he fixed his sight lined up on the rearmost Messerschmitt. Gleed was going flat out, being buffeted slightly by the 109's slipstream. He could make out the rivets on the German fighter, and see clearly the tail bracing on the German's elevators, also the black and white swastika marking on the tail fin. His thumb pressed forward on the gun button while the tiny orange light from his sight still held the 109's silhouette. The Messserschmitt took the burst, shuddered, dipped then rose as the German pilot regained control just in time to avoid hitting a line of trees. Gleed fired again, this time his bullets producing smoke from the fighter's engine while oil splashed back onto the Hurricane's windscreen. Another burst and yet another, then his guns fell silent. The 109 was now only flying at about 150 miles per hour and it had dived right down to ground level, its pilot flying violent S-turns as smoke poured from his crippled machine. Gleed left the 109 west of Alost right on the deck, its pilot obviously looking for a place to make a crash landing. He broke away and climbed making a course for Seclin. On landing he was happy to learn that Roddy Rayner had also caught a 109 and shot it down in flames. A pilot of 504 Squadron had also got airborne and bagged another 109. Gleed's 109 was credited as a probable.

Less than two hours later, at mid-day, 87 were scrambled. Near Orchies at 5,000 feet they encountered a formation of some 20 Heinkel 111 bombers. Gleed attacked one from astern, opening fire at 150 yards, closing to 25 yards. Bits flew off as Roddy Rayner flying next to Gleed made a quarter attack from the starboard side on the same bomber, firing a quick burst as he passed. As Rayner broke away Gleed closed in again and emptied his guns into the German machine. Its oil tanks erupted and some smoke issued from its engines. Oil spewed back, Figaro again being dowsed with the slimy black liquid. No attempt at evasion was made by the enemy pilot and Rayner saw the crew bale out; one wing rose upwards, then the tail as the bomber nosed over, hit the ground near St Amand and blew up.

Returning to base the Hurricanes were quickly refuelled and rearmed. The pilots grabbed a quick welcome mug of tea, wiped the grime and sweat from their faces, spoke a few words to the ever inquisitive Intelligence Officer, and stood ready. Mae West life preservers were left on, scarves were adjusted, boots or shoes made comfortable, gloves tucked in belts or pockets to be instantly ready should the call come. It came. Enemy aircraft approaching Seclin. Engines roared, pilots ran, struggled into parachutes, pulled on flying helmets, gloves and adjusted goggles. At 12.30 pm they were off once again. Over Valenciennes, flying in company with other Hurricanes, they found a dozen Dornier 17 bombers at 12,000 feet and waded in.

Gleed ordered his men into attack formation, then led them down. Tracer from rear gunners laced up towards them but was ignored. Gleed selected a target and as always held his fire until he could not miss. Closing right in behind one Dornier from dead astern he got to within 25 yards before he fired. The slim shape of the Dornier reared up in front of him, burst into flames and went down. Smoke and flame poured from the bomber, a wheel flopped down uselessly. The German pilot struggled with his controls but to no avail. Trees and hedges came rushing up at him and then the Dornier hit the ground, bounced, disintegrated and blew up. Burning petrol set a hedge alight and smoke billowed from the crash site.

Back at base Gleed found that Rayner had shot down a second Dornier while Derek Ward had knocked pieces off a third. Dickie Glyde had also blasted a Henschel 126 light observation machine he had found. After a hurried lunch of sandwiches eaten at dispersal, they waited again but not for long. At 3 pm came the order to scramble yet again. Twenty Hurricanes from the wing attacked 24 Dorniers near Tournai. Gleed attacked one from astern and slightly below, his first burst setting the enemy machine's port engine on fire. Again no evasive action was taken by the German pilot and the Dornier fell away from the formation, spiralled earthwards and hit the ground.

He looked back over his shoulder, realising he had been flying too long without doing so. His heart missed a beat. A Messerschmitt 109 was right on his tail.

Gleed found himself right in the middle of a whirling air battle, the bombers splitting up their formation and flying away in various directions as he ploughed through them with two Messerschmitt fighters on his tail. Clearing from the Dorniers Gleed pulled Figaro into a tight turn, hauling back on the stick, inching round inside his two deadly opponents. Round and round they went until one of them broke, rolled over onto its back and dived vertically. Gleed nosed down and followed, pressing the gun button as his sights came on. A large piece of Messerschmitt detached itself and flew back at him. Then tracer shells flashed over his cockpit hood as the second 109 positioned himself behind him. Stick hard over and Gleed's Hurricane went into an aileron turn, then hard over and the 109 was gone. Noting several burning aircraft on the ground below, Gleed, now unopposed in a quickly emptying sky, turned for home.

Back at Seclin he claimed one Dornier and one Messerschmitt. That made for him six kills plus one probable in two days – his first two days of combat.

1.   Wing Commander Ian Gleed DSO DFC CdeG

2. Ian and Teddy Denman in 'Spindrift' off Herne Bay.

3. The 'Moronel' which Gleed 'showed off' at Ostend and later owned.

4. Ian and Teddy – Captain and 'crew'.

As the squadron returned to Readiness state, the nearby road was now full of both refugees and retreating soldiers. Rumours were rife. Panzer divisions were closing in, fifth columnists were infiltrating everywhere, the French Army was in retreat ... etc etc. Operations ordered the squadron to prepare to move at a moment's notice. Lorries were packed with equipment, then everyone waited. It seemed to be a war of waiting and combat, waiting and combat. Along the road truckloads of wounded did little to cheer anyone.

As the afternoon passed, the sun still beating down, the pilots laid in the sun waiting for the order to either scramble or move. Finally at 6 pm the telephone rang. The squadron was ordered to Merville, forty miles on the other side of Lille. Leaving the ground personnel to move by road the pilots flew the Hurricanes to their new base. The squadron's engineering officer, Pilot Officer E.M. Sopwith, and the transport section performed a miracle of speed in packing up. From Senon the ground convoy was bombed several times but they arrived in good order at Merville. Pilot Officer Chris Darwin, whose father Major C.J.W. Darwin DSO had formed 87 Squadron in 1917, kept a small diary of the events in France in 1940 and wrote a few hurried words at this time. He had just returned from taking two ferry pilots back to the coast that morning and –

Arrived back to find there was a flap and that the squadron was moving. In the evening we were ordered to Merville. Arrived at 1900 hours – no accommodation, no food as usual. Supper in a chicken farm.

Merville was packed with aircraft. 87 Squadron had been based at Merville soon after their arrival in France in September 1939 and some of the pilots knew their way about. During the night several enemy aircraft flew over Merville but no bombs were dropped. Everyone fully expected a dawn attack but it did not materialize. Most of the pilots found somewhere to sleep, Gleed managing to get a bed in a nearby house. When he awoke the next morning it was pouring with rain.

After eggs and coffee which the lady of the house provided, Gleed went to the airfield and to the Nissen hut which 87 were using for dispersal and crew room rest centre. With rain still falling, two Hurricanes were ordered off, Roddy Rayner and Pilot Officer Peter

Comely being elected. Comely returned after shooting down a Junkers 88, but Rayner had seen nothing. The telephone rang again; two more Hurricanes ordered off. Gleed and Pilot Officer Ken Tait ran, or rather squelched to their Hurricanes and took off through the mud. They were ordered to fly south to Arras and soon clouds of rising smoke indicated they had found the town. No movement could be seen but at least the rain had stopped, making visibility better. Gleed looked at his watch; it was eight o'clock. The sun was breaking through the scattering clouds. Gleed was feeling warm and in spite of his breakfast he was feeling hungry again. Ken Tait flew up alongside and waggled his wings, the signal for enemy aircraft; Tait pointed down excitedly. Gleed looked down and saw six Junkers 88s flying towards them at 12,000 feet, but already they had seen the two Hurricanes and had begun to turn. Opening the throttle Gleed dived down upon the nearest bomber and in company with Tait carried out a Number One attack. The Junkers dived away to ground level, the two British fighters snapping at its heels like two hounds after a fox. Gleed and Tait both pulled their emergency boost control and gradually caught up with the 88, which was 'going like the clappers'. Gleed attacked again, then Tait, then Gleed, then Tait … Both pilots fired all their ammunition in four long bursts. The Junkers, badly hit, staggered and began to smoke. It was now flying at less than 100 feet and appeared to hit some high tension cables just before it crunched into the ground and blew up at a location roughly ten miles south east of Valenciennes.

Suddenly the air was full of exploding AA shells and light ground fire. The two pilots were still at 100 feet and obviously over very hostile territory. They rapidly climbed to 5,000 feet where it was quieter but then Gleed clearly heard the rattle of machine-gun fire. Gleed looked up to see five Messerschmitt 109 fighters diving down upon them, the leader already firing at them. Gleed pulled up quickly, the blood draining from his brain. Through a grey film he saw one Messerschmitt flash past him. As soon as he was able to he half rolled and dived to ground level. His head cleared and looking anxiously over his shoulder saw the 109s coming in for another attack, the leading German already snapping off bursts in his direction. Gleed dropped like a stone, narrowly missing a tree but then spotted a canal with steep banks on either side. Grabbing at this small chance he dived Figaro in between the embankments and right down onto the water. He roared along the canal, its banks rising either side of him. Bullets from the pursuing 109 (there was only one now) which was right on his tail, churned up the black water of the canal into a frothy creamy-grey foam ahead and around him but by a miracle he was not hit. He continued to race along, thankful for a sudden turn in the canal to get him away from the hail of bullets. Another turn, then another. His engine coughed as his petrol tank dried but with his heart in his mouth he quickly turned the cock of his gravity tank and the engine picked up jerkily then return to his smooth purr. Looking back he found gratefully that he was alone. He climbed away from the canal which had saved him and returned to Merville, his engine starting to run roughly again but it got him home. Ken Tait was waiting for him, equally shaken but safe.

The ground situation was now serious. Refugees were now passing Merville at an alarming rate and it seemed certain that everything was even more confused and chaotic. At 10 am a German reconnaissance aeroplane was observed in the distance which seemed an ominous sign. Then enemy aeroplanes attacked the airfield. Gleed and the others scrambled into their Hurricanes and took off amid exploding bombs. Nine Dornier 17s raced across the aerodrome escorted by several Messerschmitts. Two bombs tore holes in the ground ahead of Gleed but he swerved to one side as he left the ground then pulled up into the air. He managed to get off a quick burst at one bomber which streaked past him but more 109s were coming down and already one Hurricane was falling away shedding bits and burning. Gleed, although still fairly low, was forced to half roll and drop to ground level to evade the closing Messerschmitts. The others tried to engage the Dorniers but the 109s successfully defended their charges and made it difficult to fire accurately although one Dornier went down. The raid was over as quickly as it had begun but the Hurricanes returned to find they had lost two pilots to the marauding German fighters. It was fast becoming an absolute shambles.

No sooner were they over this shock than operations rang through to Johnnie Dewar. All available squadron aircraft were to take off to attack a Panzer Division which was advancing along the Arras

Road, following which they were ordered to evacuate Merville and return to England. Dewar had more than enough work to do on the ground in order to get the ground personnel away and arrange for the destruction of equipment which could not be taken out. He therefore ordered Gleed, his senior flight commander, to lead the attack. A French officer spoke to some of the pilots informing them that Arras and Lille had fallen and that the troops who were retreating from Senon had now reached the town of Merville. They also heard that the Germans had reached Abbeville, which if true meant that the British and French forces in and around Merville were now surrounded. Meanwhile, Gleed prepared for the strafing attack and briefed the pilots.

Nine Hurricanes remained serviceable; those others which were still in a flyable condition were flown back to England. Led by Gleed the nine took off and formed up into three vics of three aeroplanes, climbed slowly and headed for Arras. Apart from a few scattered clouds the sky was as blue and the day as warm as the previous few days. Not long after setting course, at 3.45 pm, having reached a height of 12,000 feet, Gleed spotted a Messerschmitt 110 off to one side, flying parallel with the British fighters. He ordered this to be driven off but his radio failed. He flew on, then looking back found he was alone except for the 110. Gleed dived into some clouds and so did the German but as Gleed emerged he found the Messerschmitt ahead of him. Two quick bursts sent the 110 scurrying into the clouds again and out of sight.

Still alone, Gleed turned his attention to the matter in hand. Even alone he did not hesitate. It would not occur to him to go home without carrying out the task assigned to him even without the others or without a radio. Descending to 5,000 feet he located the long, straight Arras-Cambrai Road which appeared empty until, on closer inspection, he spotted tanks and lorries parked under the trees. A half roll and dive got rid of the excess height, then he was racing along the road with his eight guns blazing. He kept his thumb down until his guns were empty, then surrounded by ground fire he pulled up and away.

Later he discovered that the others had also made strafing runs near Cambrai after some confusion. Rayner had got into a fight and also managed to bag a 109 and damage a second. The ground staff had by this time left for Boulogne, leaving just the pilots to sort out their own essential personal kit and get off with the last of the ground crews. To this end two transport planes were being flown in to pick up the last of the airmen. Meanwhile the remaining Hurricanes were refuelled and rearmed in readiness for their last flight back to England. Eventually the transports arrived and within five minutes had loaded up and taken off for the trip across the Channel.

Then the army asked for a reconnaissance to try and locate the forward elements of the advancing Germans. Gleed was not keen but finally agreed to fly out alone to have a look. Dickie Glyde and Roddy Rayner cranked his Hurricane and off he went flying towards Valenciennes which, due to the amount of extremely hostile ground fire aimed at him, he deemed to be in enemy hands. Some soldiers in field-grey uniforms came into view and as he was still being fired at decided it would be only fair to fire back. Diving down he shot up several German soldiers. Pulling up and away and followed by a good deal of AA fire he returned to Merville for the last time.

He was later to admit that his lone reconnaissance flight had scared him more than any of the big air battles in which he had been involved. As he was to describe it: 'Gosh, my knees shook!'

After waiting for final orders the remaining pilots flew off, escorting an Airspeed Ensign and two Dragon Rapides back to England. Others without Hurricanes flew back in a KLM Dakota. Johnnie Cock took off in a Hurricane which was totally unserviceable but returned safely to England. Johnnie Dewar, Chris Darwin, Watson and Rayner landed at North Weald; others landed at Tangmere while Gleed put down at Northolt. After his last lone flight, Gleed had changed into his best uniform rather than leave it behind and also, being on the small side he was able to roll up his greatcoat into a ball and place it under his parachute pack in the bucket seat of Figaro. Thus it was a smart and well turned out Flight Lieutenant Gleed who touched down at RAF Northolt and later the others admired his presence of mind in retaining his 'best blue'.

Eighty-seven's period in France was at an end. In ten days since the German attack was launched the pilots had fought themselves to a standstill. They had shot down 70 to 80 enemy aircraft between them but their own losses had been severe. Just how severe will probably never be known for several pilots had ferried out new Hurricanes in the final days and elected to stay on and fight. Many of these had died or gone missing without any permanent record having been made. Two of these volunteers who did survive and who managed to remain with the squadron after its return to England were Pilot Officers Peter Comely and Derek Ward. What records did exist were lost in the final evacuation when a truck carrying them was bombed.

Pilot Officer Chris Darwin nearly didn't make it away. Just as he was climbing into his Hurricane he remembered his diary and photograph album which were in a tent. He dashed to get them just as shells began to explode nearby. Dewar went after him but Darwin retrieved his two precious items just as a shell exploded close by. He was slightly stunned but Dewar got him back to the aeroplanes and then they both took off for home. Darwin's last entry in his diary for this period in France was dated 20 May 1940. Although he makes no mention of his last desperate moments on the aerodrome he wrote:

Hear the Germans might have got as far as Arras. Was so tired that I went into an evacuated house and slept. We have been bombed five times already. The last time when I was having lunch at the Hotel des Angiers – very frightening! Was woken up … and went out into the street. Saw one of our NCOs who said that the entire squadron was evacuating. Rushed to aerodrome and got to our machines. Flew via Beachy Head and landed at Tangmere and had a good sleep.

Chris Darwin continued to serve with 87 Squadron until he was injured in a flying accident some weeks later. He was later killed in action in North Africa in August 1942.

Ian Gleed, one friend recalls, was very angry at having been kicked out of France. Not so much for the failure of himself or the men and airmen of the BEF but of the politicians. He was determined that Britain would not go the same way as France.

CHAPTER SEVEN

Air Battles over England

After gathering at RAF Debden the remaining pilots of 87 Squadron, rested and fed, flew their surviving Hurricanes to Church Fenton on 24 May where Dewar reformed his unit. Dewar remained its commanding officer while Gleed and Bobby Voase-Jeff led its two flights.[1] Initially all the pilots were given two days' leave which Gleed spent in London seeing his family and catching up on his sleep. His sense of guilt over the failure in France remained with him for some time and for days he could think of little else but the pitiful columns of refugees he had seen.

At Church Fenton life took on a rosier hue following the final hectic days across the Channel. The officers' mess provided the luxury of single rooms although the station, far removed from their recent war, still maintained the general stiffness of a peace-time airforce which most of 87's pilots had not experienced for a long time. Most of the ground personnel had arrived back following many adventures at Boulogne although much of the equipment had been lost. Several awards were received in recognition of their work over the ten days of battle. Johnnie Dewar received both the DSO and DFC, Bobby Voase-Jeff received a bar to his DFC while Dennis David who was the squadron's top-scorer with 11 victories received the DFC and bar. Sergeant G.L. Nowell won the DFM and bar.

Several new pilots arrived to bring the squadron up to strength and the two flight commanders were kept busy in implementing training programmes. The Battle of France had been fought and lost; everyone knew what must surely follow. Gleed quickly impressed some of the newcomers when he took up a Hurricane

---

[1] Flight Lieutenant Voase-Jeff was temporarily attached to 32 Squadron until 87 Squadron was reformed.

recently patched up and repaired, for an air test. When bringing it in to land he selected 'wheels down' only to discover the undercarriage firmly locked in the 'up' position. Try as he might the wheels would not budge. Finally he was left with little choice but to bring in the machine for a belly landing. He scribbled a note of his predicament on a map, and flying low over the dispersal area he dropped his message. As he prepared to land he noted with some slight interest that the ambulance, or 'blood-wagon' as it was more usually referred to, was motoring slowly around below him, while many upturned faces of those on the ground watched his progress with equal interest. Following a trial pass he came in again and put LK-E down safely, quickly clambered out of the cockpit in case of fire but fortunately this danger did not occur.

Roland Beamont remembers this period at Church Fenton and this particular crash landing by Gleed:

> Back in the UK Gleed was at the heart of rebuilding the squadron and I well remember the intensity of his reaction when he had a belly-landing on the grass airfield following an undercarriage failure. Everything he did was underlined and emphasised in capitals and he extracted the maximum interest, excitement and enjoyment out of every situation.

Other than training and preparing for the battles to come there was little to do at Church Fenton. They could swim in a nearby river, for already the early summer was proving warm. Leeds was not far away where a few lively parties were held but the only new activity in anyway hostile was the occasional visit by German night raiders. These paid periodic visits to Hull and 87 Squadron tried their hand at trying to locate them in the darkness but without success. Pilot Officer H.J.R. Dunn was killed in a flying accident at Yeadon on 1 June which was a tragic waste. The following month came the order to move south. The squadron, now deemed fully operational once more, was sent to Exeter in 10 Group where they moved on 5 July.

No 87 Squadron was to remain in this area for the next two years, helping to protect the vital approaches to Plymouth, Portland, Bristol and the west. The squadron's morale had returned to a very high standard. Those who had already seen action in France were more than ready for another crack at the

Luftwaffe while the newcomers were all eager for the chance to have a go.

The first chance came on 9 July when Sergeant J. Cowley managed to damage a lone Heinkel 111 he found over Portland. More positive success came two days later. Johnny Dewar led two sections up during the morning finding several Messerschmitt 110s above Weymouth Bay. Four were claimed shot down, another being probably destroyed. Dewar was then promoted to wing commander and given command of the Exeter wing which comprised 87 and 213 Squadrons. His successor as squadron commander was Squadron Leader Terence Gunion Lovell-Gregg, a New Zealander, who immediately became known as 'Shovel' to his men.

Although they did not know it at this early stage of Britain's air war, the squadron would gradually fly more and more night sorties against German raiders attacking Bath, Exeter and Bristol. Ian Gleed's first experience of this came on 23 July when he was sent up and actually managed to close with a German bomber ten miles east of Plymouth. He opened fire but saw no result and so was unable to make any claim.

The squadron was kept very busy during these opening stages of what was to become known as the Battle of Britain, patrolling and often being scrambled both day and night against lone bombers or reconnaissance aircraft. Several skirmishes took place; Roland Beamont shared a Ju88 with 92 Squadron, and Roddy Rayner destroyed an Me110. Gleed took A Flight to Bibury Farm at the end of the first week of August for night fighter duties. On their first night there, enemy raiders were reported and Gleed immediately sent off aircraft to intercept. Pilot Offficer Pete Comely found a Heinkel 111 held by searchlights and shot it down; it was 87's first successful night interception.

The day battle was now hotting up and on 11 August B Flight was scrambled shortly after 10 am, being vectored onto a raid of 110+ enemy aircraft. They found the large formation of Ju88s escorted by Me109s and Me110s and waded in. At the end of the fight they could claim three Junkers and three 109s with others damaged. Unhappily 87 lost the veteran, good-looking, Bobby Voase-Jeff whose Hurricane fell into the Channel. He was due to be married on 21 August.

Pilot Officer Johnnie Cock destroyed one of the bombers but was hit by a burst from a 109 and had to bale out. Dennis David who had also shot down a Ju88, attacked the offending 109 and shot it down, then had the humorous view of Johnnie Cock swimming ashore minus his trousers. Flying Officer Dickie Glyde, a veteran of the battles in France and who had recently been awarded the DFC, was lucky to escape injury when his cockpit canopy was shattered by a bullet. Glyde's luck was to desert him two days later.

Wing Commander Dewar, with Glyde and Pilot Officer Trevor Jay, were scrambled after a Ju88 on 13 August, which the three fighter pilots despatched into the Channel. Glyde, however, caught a burst from the German rear-gunner and this gallant Australian also crashed into the sea. The battle was increasing in intensity each day and everyone knew it would get a great deal worse before it could possibly get better.

Thursday, 15 August 1940 saw the biggest air battle yet over England. The Germans, in their attempt to deliver a knockout blow to Fighter Command, launched a series of attacks in both the North-East and against Southern England throughout the day. In the south the major assaults began in the late morning and increased in intensity during the afternoon. 87 and 213 Squadrons remained at readiness at Exeter until finally the Germans came into their area during the late afternoon.

Approximately 40 Junkers 87 dive-bombers of I/StG1 and II/StG2 from their bases at Lannions, heavily escorted by Messerschmitt 109s of JG27 and JG53, numbering 60, from Cherbourg plus a further 20 Messerschmitt 110s of V/LG2 from Caen were approaching Portland. It had been a hot day, sunny with clear blue skies with only a few scattered cumulus clouds. The squadron had been warned that the Germans had been very active over Kent and things looked as if they might liven up in their direction. Then at 5.30 pm the telephones began to ring, sending them off to meet the Stukas and Messerschmitts.

Lovell-Gregg led with B Flight, now commanded by Derek Ward. Gleed followed with his flight making a quick glance back as he lifted his Hurricane into the late afternoon sky, seeing his men all racing off the ground behind him. The CO completed a circuit to allow A Flight to form up above B, then both flights climbed hard to 25,000 feet. 213 Squadron followed. At 25,000 feet the Hurricanes throttled back; the sun seemed even hotter now and Gleed for one slid back his cockpit canopy. Then they saw them. A huge formation of aircraft coming in from the south, Ju87s with the 109s and 110s stacked up above them in layers. Lovell-Gregg led them round so as to keep the sun behind the Hurricanes. The Germans were flying at about 13,000 feet, seven miles south of Portland. When in perfect position Shovel ordered the attack – it was to be his last order.

Gleed closed his canopy, then dived down with the others, unseen from the sun, going straight for the fighter escort. He singled out a 110 and opened fire. Instantly the twin-engined Messerschmitt just exploded into a ball of flames and went down. Gleed broke away, climbed again, then dived vertically to attack a second 110. The German rear-gunner fired back, sending a stream of bullets over Gleed's cockpit. A Hurricane flashed momentarily across his path, then he again concentrated on the 110, his first burst setting its starboard engine on fire. The enemy machine broke away from the formation, turned slowly over onto its back and still inverted fell away to the sea below. As he looked down he saw several aircraft splashing into the water. Another 110 loomed large in his sights – a quick burst but it was gone.

Continually weaving to and fro, his head turning constantly from side to side, his eyes ever alert to the great dangers that surround a fighter pilot in battle, he appeared to be totally surrounded by aircraft only one of which could he recognise as a Hurricane. Once again he grabbed height and seeing the main enemy formation above, continued upwards. He saw two more Hurricanes chasing the formation and latched onto them only to discover that they were not Hurricanes but Me109s. Both, however, failed to see Gleed approach at first but, when they did spot him, turned instantly to attack him. One came in to make a head-on pass while the second curved round to get behind him. Guessing the second 109 would take just a few more seconds to get into a favourable position, Gleed kept straight on and opened fire on the 109 ahead of him getting hits on its engine cowling and blasting pieces from its undersides. As the Messerschmitt neared, its pilot lost his nerve and pulled up in front of the Hurricane, skimming over Gleed's head. Gleed made an aileron turn onto his back in the classic fighter pilot fashion in order to lose height rapidly and dropped vertically downwards. The second 109 tried to stay with him but Gleed easily lost him; he eased out of his jinking dive and swooped into some clouds at 4,000 feet, then turned for home.

Gleed was credited with two 110s destroyed and a 109 probably destroyed. The other members of the squadron had also done well. Ten 110s and four Ju87s claimed as destroyed plus others damaged. Ward, Beamont, Rayner, Jay, Mitchell, David, Pete Comely and Sergeant Cowley had all scored. Gleed had seen Comely get a 110, but sad to say he was among the missing after the battle. Lovell-Gregg was also missing as well as Sergeant Cowley. Trevor Jay had baled out successfully and later Cowley was reported safe although slightly wounded having crash landed. Lovell-Gregg and Pete Comely, however, were gone for ever. Peter Comely had shown great promise as a fighter pilot and his loss was keenly felt by Gleed. Shovel, although only with the squadron for a short time, had been totally accepted and everyone felt sorry that he had been taken from them so quickly. Squadron Leader R.S. Mills DFC took over command of the squadron a few days later. He had been with the ill-fated Norwegian expedition earlier in the year and won his DFC at that time. He arrived on the 18th.

Activity around the Exeter area quietened down a bit after the 15th. Gleed and Watson chased a reconnaissance Dornier from over Plymouth and had the frustration of seeing it pull slowly away from them even though both Hurricanes were going flat out. Then they became enveloped in cloud and all hope of catching it faded.

On the 25th, Wing Commander Dewar led 13 Hurricanes away from Exeter against a reported enemy formation heading in from Cherbourg. Everyone was keyed up, for rumour had it that an invasion by the Germans was imminent. Any one of these raids might well prove to be the prelude to the expected assault upon the beaches of southern England. Only her fighter pilots could decide the issue in the air.

Over the radio came the controller's clear voice:

'Ninety plus approaching Portland from the south, Angels 15.'

The Hawker Hurricanes droned onwards and upwards. A few minutes later the controller amended the information.

'Bandits now one hundred and twenty plus, still approaching

Portland. Now twenty miles out; Angels 18.'

The squadron spread out slightly into their search formation. It was hot and stuffy and again Gleed flew with his hood open, letting the cool air blow in. The minutes ticked slowly by. It was now 5.25 pm.

'Green One to Red One – there they are straight ahead, there's hundreds of them.'

Following Tom Mitchell's words everyone saw them. Ju88s with 109s and 110s above. The German armada began at 10,000 feet and reached up to 25,000 feet. The formations met five miles west of Portland.

'Red Leader here,' came Gleed's voice over the R/T. 'OK I've got them. Come on, chaps, let's surround the bastards.'

He slammed shut his cockpit hood and dived, B Flight covering them. 13 Hurricanes against 120 enemy aircraft and Gleed was going to surround them! Looking ahead Gleed could make out the bombers below and the fighters tiered up above them. Several Me110s broke away and began to dive down towards B Flight but Gleed seeing the danger quickly turned to attack them. The 110s were coming in from the sun but as the group came within range, Gleed swung round, fired at one and saw it tumble down and crash into the sea, with, he noted, four others.

Gleed pulled round, his vision greying as the gee force took effect. As he levelled out he found himself surrounded by return fire from several Me110s which forced him to break away. Then more 110s came diving down and a terrific dog-fight began. German and British aircraft twisted and turned in the summer sky, tracer bullets and smoke trails lacing the atmosphere three miles above the earth. An estimated twenty twin-engined Messerschmitts came down. Gleed fired at one which rolled onto its back but again he had to break quickly as another 110 got behind him. Sergeant Howell saw the former 110 continue down, still inverted, towards the sea. Gleed kept his Hurricane in a tight turn. He was sweating profusely due in equal parts to the heat of the sun and the terrific exertions as the battle raged. Occasionally he managed to snap out a burst as 110s flashed in front of him but he had no chance to see the results of his fire.

The fight began to move back across the sea; the bombers, Gleed could see, had begun to turn back for France. Gleed straightened out at last, relieved temporarily not to be continually turning. A quick glance behind – danger – 109s! Two Messerschmitt 109s, the leader already pumping cannon shells in his general direction were closing fast. Gleed turned sharply, pulled Figaro round and fired as his sights came on, getting in a burst right up into the 109's tail from no more than 50 yards. Some oil splattered onto his windscreen as the 109 stalled and went down. The other 109 was still behind forcing Gleed to turn away and pull back the stick. Climbing up sharply he found he still had the 109 with him, so a quick half roll, pull back the stick and dive. Figaro fell towards the sea and left the 109 far behind. Pulling out close to the water Gleed saw several 109s above but gratefully saw they were flying south. Throttling back, Gleed gently climbed back to 5,000 feet but the sky was almost clear of aircraft. Judging too that his ammunition must be nearly finished he turned for base. Upon landing, his ground crew helped him from the cockpit.

'How many, sir?' they asked hopefully.

'Two,' Gleed replied raising two fingers, 'and another one damaged.'

The men grinned proudly. It had been another successful engagement for the unit. Three 110s, three Ju88s and four 109s plus others damaged for the loss of Sergeant S.R.E. Wakeling who did not return. Gleed himself had now reached double figures, eleven German aircraft destroyed, two being shared – and all shared with Figaro – P2798.

August ended. Patrols and the seemingly everlasting Readiness states filled the long days. At night too the pace did not slacken. Early in September several night patrols had to be flown and a few raiders were located and attacked. Beamont alone had three separate engagements on successive nights, damaging German bombers each time. A hit-and-run attack by a lone Ju88 one day caught Gleed, Watson and another pilot in the open. They were walking on the aerodrome when Watson saw a twin-engined aeroplane turning towards him.

'What on earth is it playing at?' said Gleed, then, 'Christ! it's a Ju88.'

It dropped four bombs, three of which exploded near them, but falling flat on their faces they were not hurt although some soldiers in nearby tents did suffer casualties.

Johnnie Dewar, 87's ex-CO and popular wing commander at Exeter, was killed on 12 September – a bitter blow to all who had known him. He had flown to RAF Tangmere to visit friends and while there had scrambled with others to engage enemy aircraft. He failed to return and later his bullet-riddled body was found still strapped in his parachute.

The following day, the 13th, Ian Gleed was notified of the award of the Distinguished Flying Cross. It was a fitting reward for his hard work and leadership since he had joined 87 Squadron four months previously. His next combat and his final successful fight during the Battle of Britain occurred on the last day of September.

Eight aircraft of 87 Squadron took off from Exeter at around 4.30 pm, climbing again over Portland which seemed to be the squadron's main area for hunting. It was a very cloudy day and the Hurricanes proceeded in pairs. The first two to locate the enemy raiders were Pilot Officer A.C.R. McClure and Sergeant H. Walton; there were approximately 70 bombers escorted by the ever present Me109 and Me110 fighters. McClure and Walton radioed the contact, then attacked the escort from the sun; McClure destroyed a 110 which dived away with its starboard engine in flames. Walton, however, was hit and had to bale out slightly wounded.

Gleed and Johnnie Cock were next on the scene, Cock going after a 109 which had initially attacked him but had overshot his Hurricane. He gave it a couple of short bursts and it dived into some clouds emitting black smoke. As Cock followed he came out of the cloud and almost ran into a Ju88 crossing his path. He gave it three bursts from the beam and astern. The Junkers went down with its starboard engine and fuselage on fire.

Gleed, meantime, had found Germans over the Shaftesbury area, 70 Ju88s flying in two groups in close formations with escorting fighters overhead. He made a head-on attack on the nearest, right-hand bomber, closing from 400 yards down to 25 yards, which forced the Junkers' pilot to break formation and fall towards him before it began to spiral down through the clouds right underneath him. His burst had sent 120 rounds of .303 ammunition into his target and he was credited with a 'probable'. As the 88 fell away, Gleed came under intense defensive fire from the other bombers and Figaro was hit twice as he broke away.

The long summer of 1940 came to an end. 87 Squadron had proved its worth in helping to defend the west country and its successes were many. As the autumn and winter months drew on it became increasingly evident that 87's role as night fighters must increase so that they could continue to defend this part of the country. Yet actual interceptions were not easy and many patrols proved fruitless. For his part, Gleed was keen for 87 to be as offensive as it had always been and so he put up the idea of attacking enemy airfields following discussions with some of the others. With their increasing skill at flying at night it seemed to him that it would be just as productive to attack the Luftwaffe on its home ground as to try and chase them about in the darkness over England. Group HQ approved the idea and Gleed immediately put his plans into action. Meanwhile more decorations had been received. Roland Beamont, Johnnie Cock, Roddy Rayner, Tom Mitchell, Ken Tait, Trevor Jay and Derek Ward all won DFCs, but Jay was killed in a flying accident in October when he collided with Johnnie Cock's Hurricane during a routine flight.

The squadron's first chance at an intruder mission came on 12 December; Gleed flew from the advance base at Warmwell. He crossed the Channel and patrolled in the darkness but saw nothing. Rather disappointed he returned empty handed. Twelve days later, on Christmas Eve 1940, Gleed succeeded Mills as commanding officer of the squadron. It was a proud moment. He had led A Flight since 17 May and with Derek Ward had helped to bring the squadron through the battles over England during the summer and autumn. Roland Beamont, who like Ward was to leave the squadron for other duties early in the new year, recalls Gleed at this time:

> As A Flight commander in the Battle of Britain, he seemed to us in B Flight to be running some sort of social flying club, but when he took over the squadron there was no favouritism and we were one cohesive squadron behind him. He was, of course, a fighter leader primarily, and perhaps led his administration staff a bit of a dance! We would have followed The Widge anywhere, and did.

CHAPTER EIGHT

Squadron Commander

Now in command of 87 Squadron, Ian Gleed was able to put another idea into Group. First, however, the squadron moved to Charmy Down, near Bath, where it had to continue its night interception role to protect the area. Roddy Rayner took over A Flight in January 1941 and when Derek Ward left, Flight Lieutenant E.G. Musgrove became boss of B Flight.

Fighter Command was ill-equipped to deal with Luftwaffe night raiders in the winter of 1940-41. The Bristol Beaufighters were the only aeroplanes capable of even coming close to combatting these nocturnal intrusions with any real success and they were too few in number to be really effective. Hurricanes, Spitfires and Defiants were totally unsuited to night fighting but they had to be used to fill the gap. The early weeks of 1941 were dominated by bad weather, snow covering everything including Charmy Down. However, Pilot Officer D.G. Smallwood did manage to shoot down a Ju88 on the night of 4 January which luckily he found with its navigation lights on. For his part, Gleed was hoping to continue his offensive ideas of attacking enemy bases across the Channel. His other idea was still being mulled over in his mind and that was an equally adventurous idea which will be revealed shortly. Meanwhile, Gleed had a pressing engagement; to meet for the second time his King.

Following his award of the DFC in September, he had received his invitation to be personally given his decoration from the King at Buckingham Palace on 15 October. However, this investiture had been postponed until 18 February 1941. On that date Squadron Leader Ian Gleed and his family went to the palace and it was a proud group who saw Ian presented with his well earned decoration. Another event in February occurred earlier, on the 6th, at RAF Colerne when he and Figaro flew a demonstration dog-fight against an American Curtiss P40 Tomahawk. The American fighter was flown by no less an air fighter than Wing Commander Victor Beamish DSO DFC AFC. The press were invited to the demo to see the comparison between the two fighters. Both pilots acquitted themselves well, Gleed and the Hurricane having just the edge. Several photographs of both men and aeroplanes were taken and not for the first time did Gleed's name and photo appear in the newspapers, nor the last.

Since his unproductive sortie over France on 12 December, Gleed had been pressing 10 Group, and especially the AOC, Air Vice Marshal Sir Christopher Quintin Brand DSO MC, himself a successful day and night fighter of World War One, to let 87 attack enemy aerodromes. Finally, early in March 1941, Group gave permission for 87 to plan a raid against such a target. Gleed chose Roddy Rayner to fly with him on this venture; the date he selected was 15 March when the moonlight would be favourable. On that day they flew down Warmwell in company with Derek Ward and Roland Beamont who would be the reserve pair in the event of either Gleed or Rayner having to abort.

At Warmwell the pilots were briefed. The target aerodrome was Caen, east of Cherbourg. Photographs of the base were studied and the flight plan was committed to memory. From Warmwell the French coast was 60 miles away, 60 miles of cold, uninviting sea. Caen was a further five miles inland. Then there would be the 65 miles trip back. Gleed was bubbling with excitement at the prospect of the raid; Rayner too was keen to go. The four pilots spent the evening trying not to think too much about the coming night's work, played an awful game of snooker and later tried to pass the time by reading. Finally the hours passed – it was time to go. Gleed and Rayner walked out onto the darkened airfield, Ward and Beamont watching enviously as their two companions climbed into their Hurricanes. They took off at 1.30 am for the long sea crossing to Cherbourg.

The two pilots flew low over the sea but gained height to 12,000 feet as they crossed the French coast near Point de Barfleur. Both men peered down trying to pinpoint their exact position, hoping to locate the big dark mass which would be the square shaped wood which stood at the corner of the aerodrome at Caen. They descended slightly to 10,000 feet. Then they saw it, the wood and the aerodrome nearby, just like the aerial photographs they had studied earlier. They lost height gently, the aerodrome beacon signalling to them, assuming them to be German aeroplanes coming in to land. At 2,000 feet aircraft could be seen clearly standing in neat rows, Ju88s mostly but some Dorniers and single-engined Me109s. The two Hurricanes began their strafing run, Gleed thumbing the gun button as he roared along and over the lines of parked bombers, bullets exploding and ricocheting on the aeroplanes and off the runway and hardstanding.

Then all hell was let loose as the Germans realised the danger and opened up with anti-aircraft fire. Searchlights flicked on, their silvery blue beams trying to seek out the two hornets that were buzzing dangerously above them. Both Hurricanes became illuminated briefly and the ground fire became more dangerous but Rayner and then Gleed dived down again firing at the searchlights, then curving round to fire at the parked aircraft again. As his guns fell silent, Gleed pulled up and away from the aerodrome followed by bursting shells and streams of tracer shells. It was time to go home.

Out over the Channel Gleed radioed to Rayner but received no reply. He continued home anxiously, concerned that Rayner may have been hit, but soon after he landed Rayner too came into land; his radio had packed up. In his flying log-book Gleed later wrote about the raid:

Took off at 0130 with F/Lt Rayner DFC from Warmwell bound for Caen aerodrome. Reached Caen at 0215, identified the machines on the ground to be Ju88s and Do17s. We glided down from 9,000 feet to 3,000 feet over the 'drome – no activity. We retired down moon, reduced height to 500 feet and carried out first attack, got good long bursts on aircraft parked on tarmac. As soon as I fired four blue searchlights came on, two got me, and about 20 pom-poms started firing, very unpleasant. Carried out second attack on parked aircraft, got good burst in; on turning round saw one plane burning, don't know whether Roddy or I got that one. By this time the air was full of pom-pom shells and the blue searchlights were making a nuisance of themselves so I flew down the beam and shot one out. Then

decided to shoot up the gun crews; had an amusing time
shooting at them while they shot at Roddy. Finished
ammunition and turned for home, called Roddy on R/T – no
reply. Hell ... After 50 minutes flying was over England again.
No reply from R/T ground station, so turned for coast and
landed at Warmwell. Roddy landed safely at Middle Wallop.

Their exploit gained some notoriety and a few paragraphs
appeared in the newspapers under a typical headline of the day.

WE SHOOT UP NAZI 'DROME
Two British fighter pilots who flew over to France during Friday
night saw twenty bombers on an aerodrome, and in spite of
searchlights, heavy machine-gun fire and pom-poms, they came
down low to attack. One of the pilots fired a bomber, came back
and poured bullets down a searchlight beam, hitting the light,
then shot at the pom-pom crews and saw some of them lying on
the ground.

   He made further attacks on the bombers, on a petrol tank, and
on the pom-poms.

   His companion made similar attacks and hit one searchlight
which went out.

Ward and Beamont had waited Gleed's return and listened
intently as he related his story. He later claimed a Dornier 17 as
destroyed, plus another Dornier and an 88 damaged. It had been a
complete success and Ward and Beamont would fly the next sortie
when weather and moonlight was favourable.

   Their chance came on 9 April, and their attack was directed
against Caen/Carpiquet aerodrome. They too met heavy return
fire and searchlights but strafed the field, then Beamont shot up a
train he spotted nearby. Watty Watson flew another intruder
mission on 5 May and two nights later Gleed and Sergeant
Laurence Thorogood took off from Warmwell to fly another night
mission at 11 pm, but they were not destined to carry out their raid.

   Gleed flew out over the dark sea at a height of 12,000 feet,
Thorogood doing his best to keep station with him. The miles
slipped by, Gleed thinking ahead to the planned attack. The night
was dark but a slight moon helped observation to some degree. The

two pilots concentrated on their instruments, listening for the slightest break in the smooth running sound of their single Merlin engine. They were nearly at mid-Channel where chances of survival if they came down in the sea would not be great. Suddenly a dark mass loomed up and flashed passed Gleed's aeroplane. At half way across the Channel, flying south, what appeared to be a German aeroplane, heading exactly in the opposite direction, had passed so close to him that he almost felt it. Only a few yards deviation in course and they might have collided head-on.

Gleed pulled Figaro round in a tight turn, hoping as he did so that Thorogood would not pull round too tightly after him and spin in. His eyes studied the sky ahead of him until he finally picked out the black shape again and closed with it. What was it? Was it a German? They had not been advised of any other RAF activity in the area but it could be a machine of Bomber or even Coastal Command off course or just lost. Gleed took in the shape and made out twin fins, long thin fuselage, two engines. He had seen the shape before, yes it was a Dornier, a Dornier 17z.

Mid-Channel was not the best place to have a fight, especially in the dead of night. He decided it would be far better to stay back a bit and stalk the German hoping its crew would not see him until the English çoast was reached. He would then make his attack and be in a far safer position if he was himself hit by return fire; then the German crew spotted him. The space between him and the Dornier was suddenly filled with red tracers as the German rear-gunner opened fire at him. The source of the tracers moved. The Dornier, Gleed could see, was making a left hand turn, trying to lose him. Gleed opened up the throttle and curved round after it and from 200 yards fired a quick burst, then another, then two three second bursts, the last ending when he was only an estimated 75 yards from the bomber. He had aimed at the Dornier's starboard engine and he had been on target. The engine exploded, puffed smoke then burst into flames, the orange/red glow lighting up the sky. As Gleed pulled up the Dornier began to shed pieces of burning aeroplane and went down. As he watched he saw the German pilot make a valiant attempt to pancake on the water but almost as soon as the aeroplane hit the sea it nosed forward, sent up a sheet of spray and sank, the doused glow of the flames plunging the night again into darkness. Gleed circled low seeing briefly the

Dornier's tail pointing upwards before it slipped slowly and gently beneath the waves. He noted the position – 20 miles south of St Alban's Head; the time was 11.36 pm.

Gleed abandoned the intruder mission and flew home. Thorogood had seen something go into the sea and upon reaching base was thankful to see his CO safely back. Rescue boats went out to the spot where Gleed had shot down the Dornier but no survivors were found. Everyone, including Gleed, was amazed and pleased at his good fortune in running into the German in the middle of the Channel. It was a bonus even though the intruder sortie had not been carried out. However, Beamont and Flying Officer Pete Roscoe made up for it by taking off to attack successfully Cherbourg/Maupertus aerodrome, strafing several parked Me109Fs, and destroying or damaging at least six.

The squadron had been experimenting with bombs on a couple of Hurricanes fitted with bomb racks under each wing. On the night following his Dornier victory, Gleed went out flying not Figaro but W9173, with two bombs. He attacked an airfield and dropped his bombs on a searchlight but due to haze and a particularly dark night he did not see where his bombs fell. A few nights later, 10 May, Figaro let him down – a rare occurrence. He had flown out with Thorogood for another attack with bombs on a German airfield but when he was about ten miles from the French coast his engine faltered. Checking his instruments he found that he had no oil pressure and that the glycol temperature was off the clock. He quickly abandoned any idea of flying on, dropped his two bombs and turned for home. Upon landing he found that the oil in his radiator had frozen.

Once back on the ground, he found an alert on, for it was on this night that London was on the receiving end of one of the most concentrated air raids of the war. Along with others he was sent off to Middle Wallop, flying W9154, briefed, then took off to try and intercept the raiders. He flew over burning London for some time, seeing the huge fires in and around London's dockland which were an awe inspiring sight, but he made no contact with enemy bombers, and returned to Charmy Down at dawn.

Eighty-seven's successes at night made it very difficult for Gleed to get it back onto daylight operations now that Fighter Command was beginning to look across the Channel at France and the

Luftwaffe. It seemed clear now that 1941 was not going to witness a continuation of the air battles fought in the previous year over England. The RAF was now keen to start 'dishing it out' by taking the offensive to the Germans and already Hurricanes and Spitfires, especially those in 11 Group, were flying sweeps and circus operations over Northern France. 87, however, remained in the night fighter role, but its commanding officer, always eager to get to grips with the enemy, wanted something more offensive than even night intruding. Something new and different. Something no one else had thought of. It was now that his next idea came to fruition.

Knowing the west of England and its western approaches well, Gleed's active mind had little difficulty in coming up with something new and very different. His eyes and his active and tactical imagination fell upon the Isles of Scilly, situated 25 miles south-west of Land's End, forming the most southerly part of England. In total, 140 rocky islets which cover an area of only six square miles, although only about six of the larger islands are inhabitable, with a total population of under 2,000. In this area the Luftwaffe flew unopposed from Cherbourg out to the Atlantic. Provided a suitable landing ground could be found and established, he thought that it might well be possible to maintain a small detachment there to deny or at least interfere with the Luftwaffe's freedom to roam unmolested in that area.

Gleed sent Derek Ward to the islands to look for a landing sight and he found what was in fact the only area of ground onto which a Hurricane might just be able to land. It was a cliff-top field overlooking the bay of St Mary's Island. The field was only 450 yards long, fairly level, but having a bump in the middle. It was bounded on one side by a sheer drop into a rocky sea and with a fir tree plantation on the other. Having found a base, Gleed put the idea up to Group and later persuaded them to try out the plan to place a detachment there. There was also another reason why Gleed thought the Scilly Isles attractive. The Scillies provided probably the only place in the southern environs of Britain where there was unrestricted sailing!

The first task was to practise short landings at Charmy Down, a runway area being marked out at 450 yards. Then ground crews were sent to the island to prepare for the Hurricanes and a liaison made with the local lighthouse keepers who would be the squadron's eyes so that when enemy aircraft were sighted a signal could be sent to the pilots. With no radio or radar, the lighthouse on Bishop's Rock was an important and essential part of the whole operation.

May 19 was the date set for the attempt to fly and land at St Mary's Bay. Gleed led six machines to the island, the field looking very small and uninviting to the pilots as they circled above it. Gleed went in first (he was never one for ordering others to do what he himself would not do), lowering his undercarriage and flaps, throttling back as far as he dared in order to reduce his speed to the minimum without producing a stall. Keeping away from the fir trees but ever mindful of the drop to one side he sailed in over the boundary of the field, touched down and immediately cut the engine. Figaro rolled across the grass, over the bump, and slowly applying his brakes he brought the machine to a halt.

Already the second Hurricane was coming in its pilot happy in the knowledge, as proved by his Squadron Commander, that it could be done. Hurricane number two landed safely and was soon trundling over the grass towards Gleed and the ground crews. They all got down all right even though most of the pilots needed to use the whole length of the field before coming to a halt. The ground crews immediately set about refuelling the machines while Gleed went off to inspect the site. Figaro was the first aircraft attended to and the first one ready for action.

Within minutes a red flare rose from the nearby light-house – the agreed signal for enemy aircraft in sight. Pilot Officer I.J. Badger, only recently commissioned, had only just climbed down from his own Hurricane and as soon as the shout went up he climbed into Figaro, started up with the help of two airmen and took off in pursuit. He quickly found and engaged two very surprised German seaplanes, sending one down to crash into the sea. The other quickly disappeared in cloud undoubtedly taking the bad news back to its French base that Hurricanes were about the Isles of Scilly. Badger meantime had landed again and celebrated with a nice mug of tea.

The whole episode from start to finish had happened so quickly that it surprised everyone. It certainly seemed that the venture would prove of immense interest, and a success so soon pleased everyone but the Germans.

In due course the detachment boasted a pilot's hut, a fire tender and a tent for the duty ground crew. The pilots were billeted in a boarding house in the town and during off duty hours they would crowd into its little lounge to consume large quantities of scones and Cornish cream for afternoon tea. The local inhabitants welcomed their arrival tremendously but were less enthusiastic a week later when the RAF's presence was the cause of the island's first bombing attack by the Luftwaffe. Roland Beamont remembers also that there were inevitably a few irate parents of daughters in the area after the RAF personnel had been on the island for a short while.

The Luftwaffe's swift reaction was probably due, other than Badger's quick victory, to Gleed as much as anyone. Five days after their arrival, on the 24th, Gleed and Thorogood took off to patrol north of the islands. The weather was poor, low cloud and drizzle making visibility bad. Obviously the men in the lighthouse could not see too far so a patrol had to be flown in case the weather away from the islands was a little clearer. In any event it was worth having a look. However, the weather was no better and so Gleed decided to return and land. Lowering his wheels and flaps at the beginning of his final approach ahead of him appeared, quite suddenly and totally unexpectedly, a Dornier 18 flying-boat emerged out of a cloud bank directly in front and slightly above him. The Dornier's front gunner fired his 13 mm MG131 machine gun at Gleed as the machine flew directly over him but missed. Gleed immediately pulled his Hurricane (he was not flying Figaro on this occasion) into a steep right hand turn, hastily retracting its wheels and flaps as he did so.

The Dornier went into a left hand turn, and Gleed therefore banked during his turn to carry out a beam attack opening fire at 300 yards from astern. Sergeant Thorogood had also turned to attack the Dornier and after his attacking pass he banked upwards as Gleed closed in for a second pass, getting right in behind the German. Smoke began pouring back from the Dornier's copular and Widge could see an intense fire burning inside the seaplane. Gleed fired another burst from astern and the Dornier dipped, went into a left hand turn, did a neat wing-over and crashed into the sea. As the two victorious Hurricanes circled the spot, wreckage broke up upon the surface, petrol burning furiously leaving a large black smoke column rising into the grey sky.

Four days later while Gleed and Watty sat at Readiness the lighthouse crew fired another signal flare. Both men started up their Hurricanes and scrambled (it was 7.30 pm) and headed south east. Flying at between 50 and 100 feet, the enemy raider, having been reported ten miles out in that direction, was hard to see against the water. Gleed and Watson searched the evening sky, then spotted the German 15 miles out flying away from the islands and gave chase. The German crew saw the two RAF fighters and 'poured on the coals'. Gradually the two Hurricanes caught up with the aircraft, which was now identified as a Ju88, camouflaged in sea blue/grey colours. Gleed got to within 250 yards and in the dead astern position, lined up the Junkers and gave it four short bursts. He saw strikes on the port wing and engine causing sufficient damage for the German pilot to feather it.

The Junkers swerved to the right and was so low that Gleed was unable to get his sights on so he climbed a little and carried out two quarter attacks, firing until he ran out of ammunition. The whole time the enemy rear gunner was firing back at both Hurricanes. Watson followed up with two attacks seeing his bullets striking all along the fuselage and port engine which was now pouring out black smoke and oil. As Gleed made a final pass, right on the deck, Watson lost sight of him for a second and for one terrible moment he thought Gleed had hit the sea but gratefully saw him pull up almost immediately.

The fight had carried all three aircraft 60 miles from St Mary's Bay and Gleed and Watson had to leave the German machine which was last seen still pouring out smoke and being right down on the water. It was later credited a probable although the radar plot of the German disappeared off the RAF's screens very shortly afterwards. As the light was now beginning to fail the two pilots headed for Cornwall, landing at Portreath at 8.05 pm.

These successes effectively curtailed the freedom of the skies for German aeroplanes but more especially it altered the whole tactical pattern in that area because it denied the enemy the use of the Bishop's Rock lighthouse and the islands as a navigational checkpoint for their operations in the Irish Sea. As Gleed got things organised he kept six Hurricanes permanently at St Mary's, usually three pilots from each flight spending a week or so at a time on the island. The code word for this detachment was 'Fishing'. It got to be something of a joke when newly arrived pilots to the squadron asked where such and such a pilot had gone or where was so and so going. He would be told, 'Oh, he's gone fishing old boy!'

Gleed spent time at St Mary's when he could taking his turn at cockpit readiness with the others. The local children helped to break the monotony by coming to the field on their way home from school to sit on the Hurricane's wings and chat happily to the pilots. By this time Gleed had organised his sailing activities by borrowing a four ton yacht from one of the locals. His thoughts turned to Teddy Denman, now nearly eighteen years old and Gleed decided to give his young friend a treat. Arranging to meet him at RAF Northolt, Gleed borrowed a Tiger Moth, picked up Teddy and flew him to St Mary's where they enjoyed a few days' sailing. This happened on three or four occasions while Gleed took his turn on the island, and to avoid too much suspicion and attention at Northolt he even had Teddy dress in blue slacks and shirt to look a little like an airman. However, during one trip there came a surprise visit by 10 Group's new AOC who asked whose Tiger Moth was standing on the field at St Mary's. When told it was the CO's, he asked why he had not flown down in a Hurricane. All became clear when he discovered Teddy Denman.

Meanwhile, Gleed had another job of work to do. In an ever increasing effort to help combat the enemy night raids, Turbanlite operations had been devised by someone with undoubtedly good intentions. The idea itself was simple. A twin-engined Douglas Havoc was equipped with a powerful searchlight and in company with one or two Hurricanes would take off when German bombers were reported. In theory the Havoc would locate the raider, illuminate it with a searchlight thus allowing the Hurricanes to see it clearly and shoot it down. It did not work but 87 Squadron like several other Hurricane units, had to try out the idea for some months. More often than not the sudden brilliant light from the Havoc would destroy completely the Hurricane pilot's night vision and of course the German aircraft did not hang around long when illuminated. With rapid evasive action the enemy bomber would soon be lost and it then became a more dangerous situation with one Havoc and two Hurricanes all charging about in the darkness and all pilots being temporarily blinded. 87 usually flew in co-operation with the Havocs of 1454 Flight but not a single success was achieved, and only one confirmed kill was made by any Turbanlite unit. In fact several accidents and collisions occurred before the plan was finally allowed to die.

Two pilots at St Mary's claimed a further success on 18 July when they destroyed a He111. Pete Roscoe and Sergeant Alec Thom (later destined to command the squadron) found the Heinkel at 6.45 pm, fifteen miles south-west of their base and sent it into the sea. Intruder sorties continued to be flown when aircraft were available and the weather suitable. Gleed and Thorogood planned a sortie for 6 August, and the station commander, Group Captain Hope, decided to go with them. They took off at 10 pm and headed out to the favourite German air base, Cherbourg/Maupertus. During the attack which followed Gleed encountered, what might well have been the German equivalent of the RAF's Turbanlite scheme. Gleed later wrote:

Set out with Group Captain Hope and Sergeant 'Rubber' Thorogood to ground strafe Maupertus. Lovely night, full moon, we cross the French coast at 3,000 feet and see 'drome. We peel off for first attack. I have a swift crack at two 109s sitting on the edge of the 'drome, definitely hitting them but they don't burst into flames. The usual pom-poms open up, unpleasantly accurate. I shoot at some of the gun posts, they cease firing. Lots of others shower muck at me. The only aircraft on the 'drome appear to be the two 109s so give them another burst. Then hustle round 'drome at zero feet shooting up gun posts. A fire appears on the gorund about a mile west of the 'drome.

I turn seawards, having just crossed the coast when a flying searchlight appears on my left heading out to sea at speed. I turn towards it and the light goes out. A few seconds later it comes on, on me. I give it a short burst, no results, it goes out. Can't see a thing, it comes on again, I steep turn and get behind it, give another burst, only one cannon working, light goes out, comes on again behind me. I turn for home going flat out, and weave at sea level, the light goes out. I keep going at speed, land just after Rubber at Warmwell. Group Captain Hope failed to return.

Gleed had flown Z3779 on this mission, a Hurricane he had begun to fly during July. P2798 was now getting old. He flew his faithful old war-horse for the last time on 4 August, a pleasant flight from RAF Manston. Z3779 became his personal Hurricane for the rest of his service with 87 Squadron.

Another German aeroplane, a Ju88, was destroyed by the St Mary's detachment on 16 August, this time thirty miles south of the islands and ten days later a second Junkers went into the sea just after it had flown in and bombed the town in a hit-and-run raid. A Heinkel was probably destroyed on 20 October and a marauding Messerschmitt 110 destroyed the following morning. These were the last recorded successes of Gleed's Scilly Isles venture and in early 1942 the detachment was established as No 1447 Flight, although it was still commanded by ex-87 Squadron pilots. By that time, however, its founder, Ian Gleed, had left.

He was promoted to wing commander on 18 November 1941. While undoubtedly sad at leaving his squadron with whom he had flown for eighteen months and commanded for nearly a year, he was more than happy at the prospect of leading a fighter wing. On 19 November the squadron diary recorded:

> Our CO, now Wing Commander Gleed DFC, left to take up his duties as Wing Commander Flying at Middle Wallop. He had been CO for nearly a year and had done a great deal for the squadron.

Ian Gleed was now about to enter an extremely intensive period of operational flying and be responsible for the lives of more than forty pilots. The day air-war was changing, had been changing throughout the year of 1941 and would continue to change in 1942. Since the days of the Battle of Britain the fighter pilots had been 'dragging their cloak' across the Channel and a whole new vocabulary had been brought into use to describe the types of operations the fighter pilots and the light bomber crews of 2 Group were engaged on. Gleed would soon be familiar with them all.

> *Sweep:* General term for fighters flying an offensive mission over enemy occupied territory or sea. Could be flown in conjunction with but not in direct contact with a bombing force.

Rodeo: Fighter sweep over enemy territory without bombers.

Rhubarb: Small scale freelance fighter attack on ground targets or targets of opportunity, usually flown by two, four or sometimes six aeroplanes.

Circus: An operation by bombers or fighter-bombers heavily escorted by fighters. Designed primarily to bring enemy fighters into combat.

Ramrod: An operation similar to the Circus but the principal objective was the destruction of a specific target. Fighters using cannon fire instead of bombers were termed Fighter Ramrods.

Roadstead: A fighter escort to bombers in low level attacks against enemy shipping, either at sea or in harbour. Fighter Roadsteads were also flown using fighterbombers as with Ramrods.

Jim Crow: A fighter reconnaissance sortie flown over the English Channel to keep the Channel, French coast and coastal shipping under constant observation.

The fighter squadrons, or fighter wings, had to be carefully organised. It was no use just filling the air space with aeroplanes all getting in each other's way. Careful planning took place for each operation mounted, the squadrons or wings being assigned specific tasks and areas of responsibility.

Close Escort: Surrounding the bombers.

Escort Cover: Providing cover for the close escort fighters.

High Cover: Preventing enemy aircraft positioning themselves above the close escort and escort cover fighters.

Top Cover: Tied to the bomber route (on Circus and Ramrod sorties) but having a roving commission to sweep the sky clear of enemy fighters threatening the immediate area of the bomber's course.

For larger operations, other wings might provide fighters for:

Target Support: Independently routed fighters flying directly to and covering the target area.

Withdrawal Cover: Independently routed fighters to support the return journey when escort fighters would be running short of fuel and ammunition.

Fighter Diversion: Fighter wing or wings creating a diversion, usually for a Ramrod operation.

A fighter wing usually comprised three fighter squadrons at this stage of the war; thus 36 Spitfires would normally be available. A wing could, therefore, provide one squadron for close escort, one for escort cover and a third for top cover duties on Circus or Ramrod missions. By the summer of 1941 the RAF had adopted the use of squadron sections of four machines rather than sections of three machines as used previously during the Battle of Britain. This enabled sections to be more flexible.

Gleed would also be leaving the Hurricane behind and going on to the latest version of Supermarine Spitfire, the Mark Vb. This had a speed of 370 mph at 19,500 feet, 30 mph slower than the new German Focke Wulf 190 fighters which were just coming into action, but it could turn tighter and climb faster than the 190 and the more familiar Me109F. Its armament was two 20 mm cannons (60 rounds per gun) and four .303 machine-guns (350 rounds per gun).

Gleed had already fought the Messerschmitt 109E but not the new 109F which came into service in 1941. The 109F could fly at 390 mph at 22,000 feet and could climb 3,320 feet per minute and operate at 37,000 feet – higher than the Spitfire Vb. The Messerschmitt's armament comprised one 15 mm MG151 cannon mounted between the engine cylinders, firing through the propeller spinner with 200 rounds, and two 7.92 mm (.312 inch) MG17 machine-guns mounted on top of the engine with 500 rounds per gun. It was into this scene of operations that Ian Gleed was about to take his place.

A final word from Laurence Thorogood on Gleed the CO:

'I flew a lot with Ian and due to him I probably survived the war. He was a great inspiration to us all, entirely unselfish and very brave. I have never known a better loved CO.'

CHAPTER NINE
Wing Leader

Throughout the summer of 1941 the fighter squadrons of the RAF had been taking the air war to the enemy across the Channel. Fighter Command's first tentative missions in the spring and early summer had set the pattern and had given them the confidence and experience to continue. Sweeps and circus operations were mounted.

A sweep was flown purely by fighter squadrons of at least wing strength, ie: from two to three squadrons. It was made over German-held Northern France or along the Channel coast. Circus operations comprised a small formation of Bristol Blenheim twin-engined bombers from 2 Group, escorted by 50 or more fighters. Both operations were designed to bring the Luftwaffe into combat, the circus operation being just that little extra prod, with the added bonus that the bombs would inflict damage on the target attacked, be it airfield, factory or railway centre.

Following Hitler's attack on Russia in June 1941, the pressure was continued for the air war was almost the only way the British could even attempt to hit back at Germany. RAF Bomber Command attacked Germany's cities at night while Fighter Command and the light bombers of 2 Group flexed their muscles during the day.

Fighter Command had organised its fighter squadrons into wings, each wing being commanded and led in the air by wing leaders. A wing leader, holding wing commander rank, was a very special breed of person. He was not necessarily a pilot with an impressive string of combat victories, nor did length of service count overmuch. A successful wing leader had to have combat sense, the ability to lead in the air and hold the respect of pilots on the ground and their complete confidence in the air. In the air he had to be able

*Gloster Gauntlet"
pilot "little me"   November 1936.*

*To Mummy
With love
Iain.*

5.   Gleed flying a Gloster Gauntlet at No. 8 FTS, Montrose, November 1936.

6.   Gleed seated in K7891 at Kenley, May 1937. Note 46 Squadron's markings.

7. Pilot Officer I R Gleed on 46 Squadron flying Gauntlets. Gleed walking third from left.

8. Pilot Officer Pete Comely and Flight Lieutenant Ian Gleed discuss tactics at Bibury, early August 1940. Comely was killed in action shortly afterwards.

9. Ken Tait has a pressing engagement with his flight commander. Tait, a New Zealander, was killed in action with 257 Sqdn in 1941.

10. 'A' Flight night-flyers, 87 Squadron 1940. l to r: 'Watty' Watson, 'Rubber' Thorogood, Roger Malengreau (Belg), 'Widge' Gleed, 'Harry' Tait, Roddy Rayner.

11. What the well dressed CO was wearing in 1941. Gleed with his senior flight commander, Roddy Rayner, in front of Rayner's Hurricane.

12. Ian Gleed flying 'Figaro' – P2798, LK-A. Widge flew this Hurricane from May 1940 to August 1941 scoring 20 'victories' with it.

13. *(Top left)* 'Good old A.' P2 798 with its ground crew early 1941. Note blue nose marking and two blue horizontal stripes on rudder.

14. *(Above)* Watty and Widge share a joke while at readiness on St Mary's. Note Squadron Leader's penant under windscreen.

15. Wing Leader – 1942. Ian Gleed standing in front of his Spitfire AA742, showing his personal initials IR-G, a Wing Leader's perogative.

to size up a combat situation quickly, bring his fighters into the most advantageous position and try to keep as many of his pilots alive as he could while at the same time try to inflict the maximum amount of damage on the enemy. No easy task but one which a great many men achieved with rare distinction. Some of these men became popular household names when their exploits were reported in the popular press. Douglas Bader, Bob Stanford Tuck, Johnnie Kent, 'Sailor' Malan, Johnnie Peel, Norman Ryder, Jamie Rankin, Al Deere and Johnny Johnson, to name but a few. It was, therefore, something of a reward for Ian Gleed to be made a wing leader and a recognition of his work and courage, also his undoubted courage and aggressive qualities over the last year.

Without doubt his own very individual flair and offensive spirit had marked him out as a 'press-on' type, to use a phrase very much in use at that time. Many squadron commanders were content to lead their units and carry out orders, but Gleed had done more. He had actively gone to great lengths to take the offensive, as demonstrated by his intruder missions and the Scillies venture.

Wing Commander Ian R. Gleed DFC was destined to remain in Fighter Command's 10 Group, for he was given command initially of the Group's Middle Wallop Wing. At Middle Wallop was 245 Squadron flying Hawker Hurricanes, under the command of Squadron Leader W.F. Blackadder, and 604 Squadron flying Beaufighter night-fighters, commanded by Wing Commander John Cunningham DSO DFC. However, plans were already in progress to have Gleed take over active operations from the new base at Ibsley a short distance away, although Gleed continued to live at Wallop. It would be from Ibsley that he was to lead three Spitfire squadrons known as the Ibsley Wing. Ibsley was a relatively new aerodrome situated north of Ringwood. It had been opened in February 1941 and eventually boasted three runways.

Gleed's three squadrons at Ibsley were 118, 234 and 501. 118 Squadron was commanded by Squadron Leader J.C. Carver, a pre-war RAFVR pilot and an ex-87 Squadron man who was very popular with the men under him. 234 was led by Squadron Leader M.V. Blake DFC, a New Zealander and another pre-war pilot and veteran of the Battle of Britain. 501's 'boss' was Squadron Leader C.F. 'Bunny' Currant DFC and bar. Currant was by far the most experienced of the three, having fought with distinction during

1940 and gained more than a dozen combat victories. He had taken command of 501 shortly before Gleed's arrival and had in fact been an NCO pilot on 46 Squadron with Gleed before the war flying Gauntlets. Squadron Leader Frank Birchfield took over from Blake on 29 January 1942, his flight commanders being Flight Lieutenants D.A.S McKay DFM and E.W. 'Bertie' Wootten, both experienced fighter pilots. 118's flight commanders were Flight Lieutenants J.C. 'Robbie' Robson and Peter Howard-Williams DFC.

Gleed began some early operations at the head of his wing during November, flying sweeps, sometimes escorting bomb-carrying Hurricanes – 'Hurribombers', around Cherbourg or the Channel Islands. He quickly took a wing leader's prerogative of having his personal Spitfire marked with his initials instead of a squadron's letters and individual aircraft letter. Thus IR-G appeared on his machine as well as his now famous Figaro mascot painted underneath the cockpit.

In December he led the wing on two big operations code-named 'Veracity'. This consisted of a large bombing force of 18 Short Stirlings, 11 Handley Page Halifaxes and 18 Avro Manchesters attacking the port of Brest. Gleed escorted the Halifaxes and Manchesters into the target area and they scored a damaging hit on the German battleship *Scharnhorst*. Some Focke Wulf 190s were seen but none came close enough to be a danger. All the wing returned but there were seven bomber casualties and one fighter from another wing did not get back. On 30 December 'Veracity II' took place against Brest. Gleed's wing escorted 14 Halifaxes, who to Gleed's disgust were eight minutes late at the rendezvous. Some Me109s were seen above and one aircraft which was straggling paid the price. Gleed took the bombers into the flak area and one Spitfire got hit by a bomb (which luckily did not explode) crashing right through one wing but the pilot brought the aeroplane home safely. The operation cost three bombers and three fighters.

Gleed was quickly established and accepted as wing leader and was quickly acknowledged as a brave and resourceful pilot keen to have a go at anything. One French pilot, serving with 118 Squadron, by the name of André Jubelin, who was an ex-French Navy gunnery officer turned fighter pilot, recalled in his book *The Flying Sailor* (Hurst & Blackett Ltd, 1953) the arrival of Gleed one morning at Ibsley, describing him as having '... the aspect of a destroying archangel'. Jubelin was destined to fly several missions with this archangel.

On 28 January Gleed took Flight Lieutenant Robson with him when he flew a shipping reconnaissance mission to the island of Alderney that wintry afternoon. They returned without having seen a thing of importance. The Ibsley Wing were being required to carry out more and more missions over this area of the Channel, Channel Islands and off or over the Cherbourg peninsula. It was something of a long range 'Jim Crow' task, a task which at short range was being carried out successfully by the Spitfires of 91 Squadron in 11 Group. Yet whereas 91 Squadron kept a close watch on shipping or other activities along the Belgian and Northern French coasts, Gleed's pilots had to patrol the vast expanses of the English Channel's western approaches. Flying single-seat fighters and without (at this early stage) long range fuel tanks, it took added courage to fly over this great area of very wet and uninviting sea, not to mention accurate navigation.

Setting up his wing at Ibsley kept Gleed on the ground to some degree, something which irked a flyer of his aggressive calibre. Each morning he would fly the ten minute hop from Wallop to Ibsley, plan, administer or fly on ops, then in the evening fly back to Wallop. As soon as he had all the paperwork flowing nicely in the proper directions and the winter weather eased he was able to get back into the cockpit more regularly.

Flight Lieutenant Howard-Williams of 118 Squadron had a narrow escape on 2 February, flying on a Rhubarb sortie from Ibsley. He and his number two were attacked by six Me109s. Williams was badly shot up and his number two was lost. Williams did, however, claim one of the Messerschmitts and put holes in two more.

On the 10th Gleed led twelve Spitfires of 501 Squadron plus eight from 234, as escort to four Hurribombers, through what the pilots called 'Flak Valley', the area between the Channel Islands and the coast of the Cherbourg peninsula. The task was to locate and attack a German destroyer located earlier, but as luck would have it the sea remained empty.

On the 12th came the now famous Channel Dash by the German capital ships, *Scharnhorst, Gneisenau* and *Prinz Eugen* from the port at

Brest to Norway. Owing to a combination of circumstances the ships were able to reach a point off Boulogne before being spotted by two Spitfire pilots (one being Gleed's old friend Victor Beamish, the station commander at RAF Kenley) and it took some time to organise attacks against these vessels. Gleed and his pilots were quickly alerted (as were almost every other operational unit in the south of England) and they were sent off to West Malling and briefed on what was now Operation Fuller. At 2.10 pm Gleed led one squadron out over the Channel to assist in the fighter cover for attacking RAF bombers. By this time, however, the main sacrifices had been made in attacks against the ships. Commander Eugene Esmonde of the Fleet Air Arm and his six gallant Swordfish crews had already made their almost suicidal attack. Esmonde had died along with 12 of his men and all six of the torpedo planes had been shot down by either flak or fighters. Other bombers and torpedo aircraft had made repeated attacks but all had failed. The weather was bad and the Germans had put up a mighty air umbrella over the convoy as might be expected.

When Gleed and his pilots arrived over the ships their task was to provide direct fighter cover for another strike, this time by Bristol Beauforts taking more torpedoes to the ships. All the fighter wings sent out were heavily engaged, Ibsley Wing being no exception. The North Weald, Debden, Biggin Hill and Hornchurch Wings of 11 and 12 Groups all overlapped during the mid-afternoon battle. Smoke screens were billowing away from the ships who were trying desperately to evade the torpedo planes. Above them German fighters weaved and engaged the RAF fighters as they came in. Gleed recorded in his flying log book:

Descended through cloud. After five minutes search found two large ships escorted by destroyers and small ships. Weather was low cloud with poor visibility and very low rain squalls. A 109 joined formation but dived for the cloud before it could be shot at. Lost this convoy in a heavy rain squall but found another ship with large quantities of black smoke pouring from (it) surrounded by escort ships. Nine 109s sighted, just sliding into attack when discovered nine more 109s on our tails. Luckily they must have thought us friendly as we slid off without being chased. Petrol getting low so set course for home. Tried to escort several friendly bombers; they shot at us then hid in clouds. Landed West Malling 16.00 hours.

The other two squadrons joined in the battle shortly afterwards and both 118 and 234 were engaged. Flight Lieutenant Donald McKay of 234 singled out one of the defending 109s and opened fire. Strikes flashed and splattered on the German fighter which careered away to one side and collided with another Messerschmitt, both of them falling towards the sea below. These were the only successes of the wing's action but were not gained without loss. 118 Squadron lost Pilot Officer Stone, a New Zealander while 234 lost Pilot Officers Pike and McLeod.

André Jubelin became separated from his squadron after they had left the English coast and finally broke through cloud close to the German ships. He chose to strafe the bridge of a nearby destroyer and a short while later thought he saw his squadron patrolling above. Gratefully alone no longer he climbed to rejoin them. He flew serenely along for some seconds before realising that instead of Spitfires he was flying in formation with a bunch of Me109s. He was so near to the rear one that he could not miss and opened fire from point blank range but so intent was he at getting away into nearby clouds before the other Germans saw him that he did not wait to see the effects of his fire.

In many respects it was a disappointing day. The German capital ships escaped without severe damage and the RAF and Royal Navy had for once not been able to control events in the English Channel. For Gleed, he had done his best but the final balance sheet was not to his liking. That evening he dined with Teddy Denman at the Mirabelle Club in Curzon Street, London. They had previously arranged to meet at 7 o'clock but due to the pressure of that February day it was around 9 o'clock before a tired Gleed arrived. Teddy was a little peeved at being kept waiting until his friend explained the reason for the delay. The next day Gleed dined with Beverley Nichols who later wrote an article on Gleed's experiences over the German ships.

Bad weather restricted flying during February, although Sergeant W J. Cameron of 234 Squadron managed to shoot down one of two Me109Es he attacked over Swanage on the 21st. The weather improved in early March, allowing an increase in operations for the Wing. On 8 March Gleed led a diversionary sweep over Cherbourg, taking off at 2.40 pm and landing back at 4.15; they saw nothing except for three flak bursts which came from Alderney. The diversion was in co-operation with the opening of the 1942 day bombing offensive by 2 Group further east along the coast by drawing off enemy fighters.

The following day the wing helped the new offensive in a more positive way and in one which Gleed preferred. 2 Group's Bostons from 107 Squadron went out to bomb the power station at Gosnay, Gleed's fighters flying as medium cover in support of the fighters of 11 Group. 118 Squadron flew as top cover, 501 medium cover while Gleed led with 234 as escort cover. Over Mazingarbe on the way out, FW 190s and Me109s were engaged which split up 118 and 501. Pilot Officer R.A. Newbury destroyed one Messerschmitt and Squadron Leader Currant fought three Focke Wulfs, sending one down badly hit and being credited as a probable. He was himself hit, his machine damaged and one bullet hit him in the forehead. He broke off and managed to get back to Lympne where the Spitfire turned over immediately Currant's undercarriage touched the grass – both tyres having been shot through. He was taken to Folkestone hospital (his second visit of the war) where it took two operations to remove the surplus metal from his skull.

Four days after this excitement over France Gleed flew at the head of 501 Squadron who acted as cover squadron on a Roadstead operation (an attack against enemy shipping escorted by fighters), in company with 118 Squadron, to three Hudsons of 407 Squadron, plus two fighter squadrons from Exeter. They were sent out at 4 pm to attack ships near Alderney but the weather gradually deteriorated to such an extent that Gleed decided to call off the escort and the raid, sending the bombers back and turning himself for home.

Gleed decided to have one quick look round before finally setting course for Ibsley and flew north of Guernsey. As he turned north to fly home having seen nothing in the direction of the island, he immediately spotted a twin-engined aircraft. He radioed to the rest of the squadron as the strange aircraft turned towards him, climbing at full speed in the direction of some clouds above. Whether the enemy aircraft realised he was in the near company of

12 Spitfires is not certain but at almost the same moment as Gleed identified the aeroplane as a Junkers 88, the German crew must have recognised them, though not before the crew had fired off recognition flares.

Gleed brought his Spitfire round to get in behind the Junkers and opened fire with his cannon and machine-guns at a range of 400 yards. No visible results came from this attack and he thought he must have missed. However, the German rear gunner was on the ball, Gleed experiencing fairly accurate return fire. Ignoring this he lined up the 88 again and with a little more care thumbed the button for another shot after which fire from the rear gunner ceased abruptly. The Junkers was now going flat out but Gleed and his number two, Pilot Officer R.C. Lynch, kept with it. From 250 yards Gleed gave the German several quick bursts, one of which hit the port engine which spluttered, gave off several small explosions, then caught fire. The bomber then levelled out and began to fly with one wing low as Gleed quickly closed and finished off his cannon ammunition on it, then broke away.

His number two went in to the attack from astern, also firing several short bursts of machine-gun fire from both behind and from the beam. Gleed attacked again with just his machine guns and on his final pass the Junkers nosed over, dropped suddenly and dived. The German pilot regained control lower down and dived into a rain squall and disappeared. Gleed then heard Johnnie Carver asking for help over the R/T, followed by a 'May Day' call. Gleed immediately broke off pursuit of the German machine and went down to try and locate his squadron commander who was obviously in serious trouble. It was now 5.30 pm, raining hard thereby reducing visibility down to 1,000 yards. It just had to be Friday the 13th!

Carver's squadron had turned with 501 Squadron, the clouds forcing everyone to fly low above the green/grey, white capped foaming waves. Near Alderney lighthouse a small German gun opened fire but inflicted no damage. André Jubelin, flying as weaver, had become slightly separated from the others when suddenly an enemy aircraft appeared. It was another Junkers 88, and while Gleed and Lynch were attacking theirs, this second one just popped up right in front of the Frenchman. It was slightly ahead and above him so Jubelin pulled back on his control column

and let go everything at the Junkers before yelling excitedly to
Carver that he was attacking an enemy aircraft. Yet already
Jubelin's fire had set the German's starboard engine on fire and his
Spitfire (BL264) was surrounded by return fire from the enemy
gunner. Then Carver, having quickly turned into the attack, made
his pass on Jubelin's port side. Jubelin saw the German gunner
swing his gun in the direction of Carver's Spitfire (W3143). The
German's first burst hit Carver's engine, smashing the coolant
tank. Jubelin saw Carver's machine, enveloped in white smoke and
spewing out glycol, drop back and begin to fall away. Jubelin then
set the port engine of the 88 on fire and the bomber dived away out
of control to completely vanish in low cloud. Although low on fuel,
Jubelin climbed to radio Carver's position so as to establish a fix for
his CO, then flew home.

Carver had in fact recovered from his dive and levelled out but
his cockpit was full of glycol and his engine temperature quickly
rose alarmingly; then the engine began to knock dangerously. He
managed to climb to 2,000 feet where he baled out. Carver hit the
water at 5.28 pm according to his wristwatch which stopped as he
went into the sea. He scrambled into his dinghy to begin an
agonising 57½ hour ordeal which finally ended in the early hours of
16 March when in pitch darkness he found himself in the middle of
a merchant convoy. By blowing on his rescue whistle he was heard
by a helmsman on the escorting Hunt Class destroyer HMS
Tyndale. He had baled out off Cherbourg but was picked up only
seven miles from Portland.

March 1942 was proving a busy month for Ian Gleed and his
wing. A sweep over Cherbourg on the 14th was followed two days
later by an escort to five Lockheed Hudsons, again to attack ships
located west of Guernsey. It was the wing's longest ever sweep –
over 300 miles. Gleed led 118 at medium cover, 501 close escort and
234 high cover. Gleed later recorded:

Went to Les Sept Isles. 234 lost Wing whilst investigating objects
that were rocks. Two 109s seen in distance. Landed at Exeter
with 28 aircraft. Weather very bad, cloud on deck in places. Four
of 234 landed Bolt Head after 2½ hours airborne, 4 crash landed,
one killed. Impossible weather and no homing.

The 23rd was more fruitful. It was 7.30 pm in the evening with a greying, hazy sky when enemy aircraft were reported approaching Portland. Gleed had flown back to Wallop for his evening meal in the mess when the alarm was raised. It almost seemed like the Battle of Britain again with him dashing to the airfield, ordering his Spitfire started up. Tying his scarf around his neck he grabbed his helmet and goggles, climbed onto the wing of Figaro and

The hunting ground 1941-42

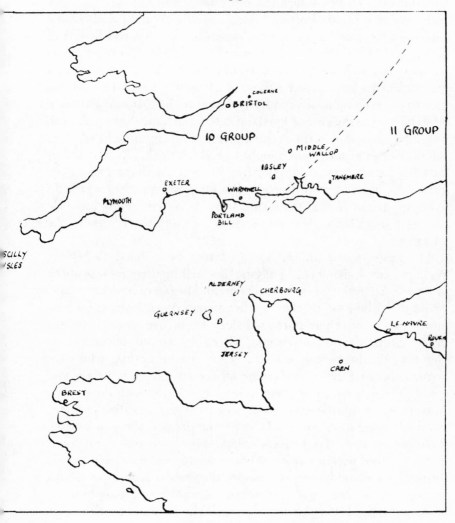

clambered into the cockpit. Helped by his mechanic he went through the pre-take off procedure then taxied out to the runway. Within minutes he was off the ground and turning towards the south and the sea, climbing hard, and knowing that 118 Squadron had been scrambled from Ibsley.

Gleed continued to climb hard, keeping a sharp look out in the hope that he would see 118 coming up from Ibsley, or in any event he should meet them near or over the coast. Over the radio came the controller's voice informing him that the enemy aircraft were still coming towards Portland. Both Middle Wallop and Sopley controls were monitoring their progress as they approached. Still no sign of 118 Squadron and the minutes ticked by. Soon the hands on his wristwatch were nearing eight o'clock. Again the radio told him the enemy were near Portland at a height of 16,000 feet. At this time in the evening it was naturally darker to the east as night came on so he flew to the east of Portland Bill in the hope that his Spitfire would be concealed in the evening gloom. Still climbing he reached 18,000 feet at exactly one minute to eight o'clock. Three minutes later his expert eyes picked out five Junkers 88s flying in *Schwarm* formation, ahead and to starboard of his position. They were still flying on a northwards track and were 2,000 feet below him. He could see them quite clearly against the sea and partly against the afterglow.

As he positioned himself for an attack he radioed to Middle Wallop control giving the 'Tally-ho' and telling them he was about to attack. Then the Germans saw him and began to break in panic. As he dived he saw another Spitfire swoop down from above and attack them from their starboard side. As the five enemy bombers broke formation and separated, Gleed joined in, selecting two Germans on the port side of the scattering formation, who were turning towards the west. Having all the advantage of height and speed, he easily overtook them in his dive, closing with the leading Junkers which now seemed to be going flat out and diving. Gleed steadied himself; at 200 yards' range he pressed the gun button. Reacting swiftly, the Junkers' pilot climbed steeply and for a moment Gleed was in danger of overshooting his target. He rapidly throttled back and swung out to port, then neatly side-slipped back and opened fire from the port quarter, hammering a long burst as he closed from 150 yards to 50 yards. The 88's starboard engine burst into flames while strikes sparkled all over the bomber's fuselage.

The German machine's speed dropped away rapidly, so quickly and suddenly that Gleed was in danger of colliding with it. He pulled his Spitfire into a steep turn to port and looked down to watch the bomber go down in a glide over the sea to the west of Chesil Bank, flames and burning petrol pouring from the shattered engine and wing. At 4,000 feet a mile or two west of Portland Bill the Junkers became completely enveloped in flames, then slowly nosed forward to dive vertically towards the sea. Highly satisfied, Gleed turned for base, landing at 9 pm.

A few days previously the boys had quite a party at Ibsley which turned into a very reasonable thrash. It was at the total expense of the film makers and crew following the successful completion of the film *First of the Few*, the story of R.J. Mitchell and the birth of the Supermarine Spitfire. Some of the scenes had depicted some of the wing's pilots including Bunny Currant, Robbie Robson, David Fulford and Peter Howard-Williams. The film starred Leslie Howard, David Niven – and the Spitfire!

On 2 April Gleed led six Spitfires from 501 plus six from 118 on a shipping reconnaissance over Cherbourg, reporting on his return that two armed trawlers were sitting in the harbour with larger ocean going vessels nearby. Shortly afterwards a strike was organised against them. Five days later Flight Lieutenants Robson and Jubelin of 118 Squadron, at cockpit readiness, were scrambled at 1135 am when an unidentified aircraft was reported over the Channel at 20,000 feet ten miles south of Portland. After climbing hard they spotted an aeroplane high above heading south, the two pilots chasing after it. The 'bogey' had the advantage of height and speed over them but Robson and Jubelin, with throttles wide open gradually began to close the gap. Finally they got within range. It looked like a 109 but Jubelin was unsure, so he climbed a little and recognised it as a Spitfire. In his book, Jubelin records that it turned out to be a wing commander out for a morning spin and he hoped that the man would get a dressing down appropriate to his rank, for presumably not having proper authority for his flight nor letting 'ops' know that he was out on his own. However, perhaps Jubelin was just a little put out at having to rush after this machine and be put in the invidious position of nearly shooting down a friendly Spitfire and its pilot. This is probably why he did not record, as his Squadron Form 540 does record, that the offending wing commander was none other than their own 'Wingco' – Ian Gleed! However, it was with Jubelin that Gleed had a scrap with enemy aircraft on the 16th.

Widge was away from Ibsley for a couple of days, attending a Higher Commanders' Course at RAF Old Sarum on 8/9 April, returning full of ideas for future operations. On the 15th Gleed led the wing on 10 Group Circus Number One (10 Group were now organising their own circus operations as 11 Group had been doing since the previous year). 118 flew as close escort to nine Douglas Bostons bombing Cherbourg. 234 and 501 flew above and above them cruised two Polish Spitfire squadrons. Heavy flak was experienced over the target and 234 were attacked by enemy fighters and lost two machines.

After the battle Gleed dropped down to search for a pilot in the sea and later recorded in his log book: 'Nearly got shot down later when searching for a pilot in the sea,' but how or why we do not know.

The next day Gleed led 118 Squadron and wing as escort to six Hurribombers attacking Maupertus aerodrome. They had a brief exchange with some enemy fighters but no claims were made. One Hurribomber went into the sea streaming glycol and one Spitfire went down in flames. The Hurricane pilot got into his dinghy and several Spitfires, including Gleed, stayed over him for as long as possible but he was not rescued. One thing Gleed did learn for certain was that '... 190s definitely got cannon!'

Later Gleed put himself on the readiness rota. This job could have been left to junior officers but Gleed continued to believe that he should share every job with his men – even the often boring job of cockpit readiness. When the alarm sounded he took off in company with André Jubelin (who was flying Spitfire AA752) shortly after 4 pm. High over the English Channel they found three Messerschmitt 109s, and in a brief scrap the Frenchman severely damaged one and scored hits on a second. André Jubelin was awarded the French Croix de Guerre on 30 April.

The day after Gleed and Jubelin's fight with the 109s was a busy one for the Wing and for the Royal Air Force. This Friday saw the daring daylight attack on the Messerschmitt factory at Augsburg, deep in enemy territory, by a force of Avro Lancasters led by Wing Commander J.D. Nettleton. Raids by light bombers of 2 Group acted as diversions. Gleed's own wing flew a sweep over Cherbourg, taking to the sky at 9 am and landing back at 10.25. All three squadrons took part and sweeping south of Alderney, three Me109s were sighted.

It was a hazy morning, with 5/10ths cloud to 10,000 feet. Gleed spotted the three Messerschmitts flying towards the Spitfire formation from below. He immediately turned to starboard and commenced a diving attack. The 109s began to climb steeply and also turned, frustrating Gleed's attack as he failed to get within range. Therefore, he ordered Bunny Currant and 501, being the medium cover squadron, to have a crack at them. Seeing 501, the 109s started to turn towards them which enabled Gleed to climb hard and close with the three Germans.

Seeing the danger from both sides, two of the Messerschmitt pilots dived away and 234 Squadron, the high cover squadron, peeled away after them. The remaining 109 was surrounded by Spitfires. Currant opened fire at it and so did Pilot Officer Newbury, Pilot Officer Drossart, a Belgian pilot, and Sergeant Rocovsky. Gleed also came in and fired too, observing hits on the Messerschmitt's belly and centre fuselage. After his attack the 109 stalled and fell away vertically. Gleed also saw Currant's fire splatter over the German's fuselage. Sergeant Rocovsky followed the 109 down to 8,000 feet and reported it still diving and smoking. Gleed was of the opinion that the 109 pilot had been hit, possibly killed, but as it was not seen to crash they could only claim it as a probable. 234 had managed to engage the other two 109s, Flying Officer B. Wydrowski claiming one as damaged.

Reforming, Gleed led his Spitfires back across the Channel but were followed by other enemy fighters. Fuel was running low so they could not afford to engage but when the English coast came into view, Gleed turned towards them. He put his Spitfire into 12 boost and 3,000 revs: but the Germans turned back and he was unable to get nearer than 600 yards but it put the wind up the 109s and Gleed saw them begin to leave smoke as they too applied full boost. Being unable to get closer Gleed decided to fire anyway to help the Germans on their way. He raised the nose of the Spitfire to allow for various degrees of bullet drop at this range and keeping his thumb down, he emptied his guns in the direction of the 109s before he lost flying speed and stalled away, but saw no visible results from his fire.

Further east 2 and 11 Groups had flown a diversionary attack against a power station near Rouen and nearby shipyards while other bombers attacked Calais.

Later that afternoon 10 Group organised a circus operation to Cherbourg, the Ibsley Wing escorting twelve Douglas Bostons from 107 Squadron in an attack on the harbour. Gleed led 118 Squadron out at 4.05 pm, the afternoon proving fine although still hazy. 234 Squadron flew above as cover escort.

Gleed's original briefing instructed 118 to wait for the Bostons outside the harbour's flak radius but in the air he was warned by the Middle Wallop controller that enemy aircraft were coming in from the south-west and from above. Gleed, therefore, led 118 into the flak but kept well to the south of the approaching Bostons.

After having made their bombing run the Bostons turned north with Gleed and his pilots weaving behind and slightly above. It was then that he saw enemy fighters – nine Me109Fs – climbing up from the right. One Messerschmitt levelled out and attacked the Boston nearest to it. Immediately Gleed dived Figaro and snapped off a one second burst from the German's quarter but missed. It was enough, however, to make the 109's pilot break away, but towards him, roaring in over Gleed's cockpit a second or two later. Already a second 109 was attacking the Boston. Gleed was in an excellent position to attack this Messerschmitt and opened fire from 150 yards. He saw his bullets strike just forward of the 109's cockpit and then the German broke off the attack, nosed over and dived vertically, pouring out smoke and shedding pieces. The high cover squadrons of another wing saw the 109 fall away and later reported that the German pilot baled out just before his fighter crashed into the sea just north of Cherbourg.

The press reported the day's operations in some detail. Nettleton's raid had suffered severe casualties although some of the Lancasters had reached the target and bombed the Augsburg plant. His gallant effort was later recognised by the award of the Victoria Cross.

Ten Group too received its share of the publicity and it was stated that altogether between 500 and 600 RAF aircraft had taken part that day in sweeping in total a 200 mile arc between Calais and Cherbourg. Two German aircraft had been destroyed and apart from the Augsburg raid, three RAF aeroplanes had been lost. Ian Gleed was interviewed as a wing leader who had been involved in the fighting and who had shared in the successes. They questioned him about the raid on Cherbourg and his answer was quoted in the press: 'One of our bombers was shot down but I got the man who did it.'

The following day's operation was not a success, at least not the latter part of it. Gleed led 234 Squadron as high cover to 118 and 501 in a sweep once again over Cherbourg but nothing was seen. Returning home Pilot Officer Cameron (in BL693) and Sergeant Fairman (AA938) collided west of Ibsley, near Ringwood. Cameron managed to bale out of his crippled Spitfire but Fairman was not so lucky and was killed. Both pilots were at 1,000 feet and it all happened directly in front of Bunny Currant's squadron who were following 234 home. That afternoon they escorted six Hurricane bombers in an attack on their favourite aerodrome at Maupertus. Four 109s made a quick pass but caused no harm.

Four days later, 22 April, Squadron Leader Johnny Carver was discharged from hospital. He had been recuperating from his ordeal in the Channel at the RAF hospital at Torquay, the same hospital Gleed had convalesced in following his crash in 1940. Immediately, Carver visited the company that made the dinghy in which he had sat for 57½ hours, Messrs P.P. Cow & Co., to thank them for their good work and to tell them how much RAF pilots valued the reliability of their product. The visit went down very well, Carver being received warmly by both workers and management. After this very worthwhile visit Johnny Carver returned to his command; everyone was happy to have him back.

That same day Gleed led all three squadrons as high escort to Hurribombers attacking Maupertus once again, and as close escort to the Fairwood Common Wing. Two 109s were seen in the air but they wisely decided not to mix it with several squadrons of Spitfires, but when 10 more showed up there was a brief exchange before the Germans broke off and '... ran for it'.

CHAPTER TEN

The Widge

Ian Gleed was proving to be a most competent wing leader as well as an inspiration to the pilots under his command. Bunny Currant, an equally exceptional fighter pilot and himself a future wing leader, remembers Gleed vividly during that early summer of 1942:

> He was I would unhesitatingly say one of the most courageous men I've ever had the privilege to know. He may have been tiny in stature but by God he had a big heart and seemed not to have any fear. He was unmoveable and unflappable with a modest, unassuming manner and always thought for his pilots and for the ground crews and staff. A caring man, I remember him warmly with gratitude. A pocket size man with care for others and courage beyond compare.

It was about this time that the famous writer, playwright and novelist W. Somerset Maugham, whom Gleed had known, stayed with and sailed with before the war, had his latest book published in England. It was entitled *Strictly Personal* (William Heinemann & Co, 1942) and dealt with Maugham's thoughts and experiences of wartime France and Britain during the first fifteen months of the war. In dealing with his impressions of Britain's gallant airmen, Maugham, at this date aged 66, wrote about one young flyer he had been particularly impressed with. Although in the book he does not mention the pilot by name it was Ian Gleed. Naturally they had kept in touch, Gleed occasionally seeing him at a party or other function, Maugham having learned more of his young friend, and his achievements as an air fighter:

'I thought I need not concern myself about the airmen. Their daring, their coolness and presence of mind, their indifference to odds, their endurance, had been shown in a hundred air battles and praised by the press of the whole world. I had myself known several members of the RAF, and when I looked at their youth, my heart was wrung because, with all their life before them, they had to take such fearful risks. Some of them showed cheeks so smooth that you felt a safety razor was only recently a necessary part of their equipment; and yet they were so light-hearted, so gay, reckless yet confident in their skill, boys in appearance but men in experience, wily and knowledgeable, with old heads on young shoulders, that it was not enough to be proud of them; I was filled in their presence with a great humility.

'I knew one somewhat more intimately; he was a little older than the others, twenty-four, and quite a little chap, not more than five foot four, I should guess (just the right height for a pilot, he said), jaunty, with a care-free look in his impudent blue eyes. He had crashed early in the war and had nearly broken his neck, but after a few weeks in hospital and a niggardly leave, had gone to work again. He came to see me soon after his return from France, and he had grim stories to tell of how the French, after their surrender, had tried to prevent the British planes from getting away, how they refused to give them gas and oil, and how they had driven trucks over the airfield to prevent those whose tanks were full from taking off – bitter, shameful stories, but not such as it is any use to dwell upon.

'Shortly before, he had had a scrap with two German planes, one which he brought down; a lucky shot pierced the oil tank, and so close were they that the oil splashed over his own plane, with the result that he could not see through his windscreen, but had to guide himself home by looking backwards over his shoulder.

'"They were rather interested in that when I got in," he said. "An expert came and examined the oil, and he said it was rotten – we wouldn't use oil like that in a truck."

'I asked him if he wasn't scared.

'"Not then," he said. "I've never been scared in a scrap – it's too damned exciting." He thought for a moment. "But I'll tell you when I have been scared. When I was on a reconnaissance by myself. When you're up there all alone, hour after hour – Gosh, my knees shook. You feel there's no one in the world but you, and the sky looks so damned big. There's nothing to be afraid of really, I don't know why it should make you feel funny."

'"Infinity," I suggested.

'He was a jovial, cheery soul. He was in tearing spirits because he had two days' leave and was determined to have the time of his life. He was full of plans for the future. After the war was won, he was going to buy a sailing-boat, forty foot long, and sail with a friend to the South Seas.

'"It doesn't cost anything to live there, does it?"

'"Not much," I answered.

'"I shall have a grand time."

'I never saw him again. Perhaps he knows now that there's nothing so frightening in infinity after all.'

Not long after Maugham's book was published, fellow writer and mutual friend of Ian Gleed, Hector Bolitho, read it and recognised Gleed from the above extract. In his diary for 23 April 1942, Bolitho jotted down these facts. Bolitho was an intelligence officer with the Royal Air Force in 1942, a job which brought him into contact with many flyers. In his diary he recorded many events concerning these men and their exploits about which he had to write for the Air Ministry *RAF Journal* which he had personally created. This diary, in part, was published in 1955 in a book entitled *A Penguin in the Eyrie*. (Hutchinson & Co, Ltd, 1955). In his diary Bolitho wrote:

'The pilot is Wing Commander Ian Gleed DSO DFC. He has brought down thirteen enemy aircraft and is now OC Flying at Middle Wallop, in Wiltshire – which means that he controls the daylight attacks by Spitfires on enemy aircraft assailing our coast.

'Soon after he joined the RAF, in peace-time, he used to come and see me at my house in Essex. The picture I suddenly recall is of myself at a desk, before the window, looking out at Ian playing with my Dalmatian on the lawn. They were both at the puppy-dog stage and had much in common. His enthusiasms were enchanting: his escape from flying was a little sailing-boat, the modest forbear of the forty-foot sailing boat in which he will seek freedom in the South Seas, when the war is over.

'I closed Mr Maugham's book at page 137 and telephoned Ian Gleed, at Middle Wallop. Yes, he would be delighted to see me. If I arrived by the afternoon train, he would meet me and we could dine at the Haunch of Venison, in Salisbury, that night.

'So I travelled down from London to see what had happened to the boy who had played on my lawn. We dined at the Haunch of Venison, off legs of chicken that seemed as old as the oak beams above us, and we talked. Ian's merriment made it hard for me to believe in the thirteen combats with German aircraft. When we relaxed in seriousness, over our pallid coffee, I realised, in the depth of his voice and the quiet of his mind, that there was wisdom behind the laughter.

'After dinner we strolled along the bank of the Avon, to Harnham, and we did not speak of war all the way.

'Next morning, I walked with Ian to the aerodrome, to see his new Spitfire; past the bombed skeleton of a hangar – a great dinosaur of steel bones, with birds flying in and out. The Spitfire was fresh from the factory and ready for battle: Ian stroked its fuselage with the palm of his hand. Five airmen were working on the aircraft, tinkering and screwing and painting, poking their heads into its mysteries so that their behinds and legs hung in mid-air. We went again in the evening: the five were still working and one of them was painting Ian's mascot on the body – the cat from Pinocchio, smashing a swastika with its paw.

'We walked back to the mess – a calm, lovely, Wiltshire evening; great shafts of light from the setting sun, stillness and peace. Next morning I slept late and Ian was already flying over the French coast when I was shaving.

'On the third day at Middle Wallop I listened while Ian briefed the Spitfire pilots before he led them on their task for the day. I realised the incredible authority that has developed in his little frame: he sat on the edge of a table while he gave his orders and his shoes did not touch the floor, yet he seemed to be expanded by his own will. His quiet, still-young voice never hesitated as he told his men exactly what they were to do, what they might expect from the enemy, and where.

'The pilots looked up at him, tense, leaning forward to absorb every word that might increase their chance of survival and return. Then Ian swung his feet, jumped from the table and walked over to me. I went to see him off in his new Spitfire; then I spent the hours in his absence watching a tough football match, and writing at a desk.

'When Ian returned, he washed and changed, then said, in a quick, rather harsh voice, "Come for a walk." We went, but he was mostly silent. After about an hour he said, "I lost two of my boys this morning; the Messerschmitts came down on them out of the sun."

'We dined, and afterwards we sat in his room, drinking and talking – of his wish to be a writer, of his dream of the forty-foot boat and the South Seas. Then he said, "I've grown up too fast. Forget all that you saw today. I want to be treated as if I were a boy again: it is something I have lost, and I want it back."''

The operation of which Gleed spoke to Bolitho occurred on 25 April. The 24th and 25th were not good days for the Ibsley Wing. On the afternoon of the 24th Gleed led 118, 234 and 501 Squadrons on a sweep along the French coast to Berck-sur-Mer where the Luftwaffe had a figher base, and where Gleed had landed after his first combat in May 1940. Seven of his pilots became separated from the main formation during a turn and were bounced by about 40 Focke Wulf 190s which dived down from above and behind. Before they knew what had hit them, four Spitfires went down from 234 Squadron who had been split up; Flight Lieutenant Watkins, an American, Pilot Officer Svendsen, a Danish pilot, and two Canadians, Flight Sergeant Fisher and Sergeant Machin were lost. The wing had been at 25,000 feet in company with the Tangmere wing. Gleed commented in his log book after the fight, 'Bloody fast aircraft the 190s.' The next day was not any better.

The first mission of the day was a 10 Group Circus (Number Four). Gleed later wrote:

Set course 0904. Reached Cherbourg and bombed from E-W; intense heavy flak, the first hitting a Boston which force landed in France. 12 109Fs attempted to attack bombers and escort in flak area. I attacked one of these and damaged it, last seen by Boston gunners diving vertically with smoke pouring from it. The high cover Polish Wing was attacked over target but EA ran away. We lost two fighters and one Boston.

Gleed had turned to attack these 109s as they came in at the bombers and fired a one second deflection burst from 150 yards but several more 109s then came between him and the other bombers and he was unable to pursue his victim. Sergeant Verrier, rear gunner in one of the Bostons, later confirmed seeing the 109 going down upside down leaving smoke and diving vertically.

No 402 (Canadian) Squadron substituted for 234 Squadron for the second sortie of the day for a wing offensive sweep over Cherbourg's peninsula. They met the enemy over Barfleur and Gleed wrote:

Led 501 Squadron on sweep of Cherbourg peninsula. Attempted to attack eight EA and was jumped by 6 more. Was attacked all across the Channel by 109Fs. These EA continually carried out dive attacks on the formation. Five of our aircraft were shot down, we probably (got) one. About 6 FW190s attacked the formation south of Swanage. Bad show.

This showed an unusually aggressive attack and pursuit by German fighters whose persistent attacks caused severe losses to the Spitfires. It was rare for them to chase RAF fighters as far as the English coast. 501 lost four pilots, two being great pals, the two others being Czech pilots.

During the night of the 26th, Gleed took off in a Hurricane II when night raiders were reported, and found a Dornier 215. His own comments seem to sum up his feelings:

Took off for fighter night, saw aircraft over Salisbury; as I was approaching to attack one engine caught fire; followed EA for 5 minutes when it crashed. *Did not fire. No one claimed it. Bloody annoyed.*

He was back in action the next day leading the wing on an 11 Group circus to Ostend. Ibsley Wing were detailed as target support. They were received with heavy flak from Dunkirk and as the bombers were late the Spitfires had to orbit above Nieuport. Later they escorted both bombers and close escort fighters out of the target area and covered their withdrawal. On the last day of April Gleed led his men on yet another sweep of Cherbourg.

On 1 May 1942 Gleed flew with 501 Squadron and the squadrons of the Tangmere Wing during a sweep over the Pas de Calais but the Luftwaffe declined to put in an appearance although some smoke trails were seen high above. Three days later The

Widge made a short radio broadcast for the BBC which was entitled Fighter Sweep. It lasted 2½ minutes and was heard over the air at noon on that Monday. The following afternoon he was leading his wing from Tangmere over France and made his final combat claim in Europe.

Leading 118 and 501 Squadrons as top cover to the Spitfires of the Tangmere Wing, again sweeping the Pas de Calais area for an 11 Group rodeo, Gleed looked down on the panoramic scene of Northern France from 24,000 feet – a scene he had known so well for so long. It was a fine warm day, the visibility unlimited. Nearly two years earlier he had been flying and fighting for his life not so far from this spot when the odds against the RAF had been far greater than they were now. How long ago that all seemed and how far he had come since those dark days of the Battle of France. He had proved himself then and more than proved himself since.

Crossing the French coast at Hardelot the Spitfires flew inland. Ten miles into France fifteen Focke Wulf 190s were seen ahead and below passing almost leisurely across their front from left to right. Gleed immediately gave quick, crisp, concise orders, then pushed his control column forward and led 501 Squadron down to the attack. The Spitfires were only 800 yards away from the enemy fighters when the German pilots saw them and all but one quickly half-rolled and dived earthwards in a rare but understandable state of panic. The sole 190 remaining, the pilot of which Gleed was later to describe as 'Leutnant Prune' (referring to the supposed German equivalent of the RAF's most famous 'finger right in' cartoon character Pilot Officer Percy Prune), continued to fly along straight and level. He was obviously unaware of the imminent danger and also that all his pals were rapidly becoming mere dots against the distant patchwork of the French countryside. Either they had not warned him or, more probably, his radio was not working or not switched on.

Gleed was not going to let this one off the hook and came curving down on the German's starboard quarter, closed right in astern of him and fired a two second burst. He let go between 300 and 400 yards from it, seeing strikes all over the sea grey coloured Focke Wulf which then half rolled as if it too was going to dive away in regular fighter pilot fashion but then continued to fly, still in a more or less straight line of flight, but completely upside down.

Gleed had fired 83 rounds of 20 mm cannon ammunition and 189 rounds of .303 bullets from his machine-guns and as he was deciding whether to attack again, the 190 simply fell out of the sky and began to pour out smoke. Grey smoke streamed from the falling fighter and it was Gleed's impression that the pilot was either dead or wounded. As the 190 fell he lost sight of it although his Red 3 saw it continue down vertically still leaving smoke until he too lost sight of it close to the ground. Therefore, with no witness to its end the wing commander was only able to claim a probable. Several other 190s were later seen but they showed no inclination to join combat with the Spitfires.

On 9 May, the pace continued. Gleed recorded:

Led wing formation on Tangmere Wing as top cover for 11 Group circus. Rendezvous Beachy Head, set course 1306. Crossed coast at Hardelot; reached position 27,000 feet, 10 miles N of St Omer. 30 plus FW190s were seen 2,000 feet above us to the N, while a further 30 plus attacked 118 Squadron from the S. The wing assumed a defensive circle. 118 Squadron was soon split up in ensuing dog-fight. 30 FW190s continually circled above without attacking. Wing managed to ooze out via Gris Nez. Five casualties, enemy NIL, although one EA was destroyed but no living pilot claimed it! Heavy flak from Calais.

Six days later, 15 May, Gleed led all three squadrons together with 66 Squadron's Spitfires from Exeter, as escort to eight bomb-carrying Hurribombers of 175 Squadron against three ships which had been spotted off Cherbourg. The target proved to be three minesweepers and the weather was fine with no clouds in the sky. So as to gain maximum surprise Gleed led the whole formation out at wave-top height and if no enemy aircraft were present above the ships he would lead the Spitfires in on strafing runs in order to suppress the ships' return fire thus allowing the Hurricanes a less dangerous task.

As the wing sighted the Cotentin peninsula, they divided into groups, each group ready to fly straight in to attack the minesweepers which then appeared on the horizon. As they drew near Gleed ordered the groups to fly at different heights from between 20 to 500 feet in order to spread the return fire and confuse the gunners. He yelled encouragingly over the radio:

'Hello boys, now for it. There they are. Between the masts – its a piece of cake. Come on chaps, hold your fire till the last second. In with you.'

By now the minesweepers were throwing up a curtain of light flak but the Spitfires and Hurricanes came in steadily, Gleed and one squadron heading for the centre ship. They raked the decks of the ships with both cannon and machine-gun fire, and the Hurricanes let go their bombs. As the attack ended one minesweeper blew up, a second burst into flames while the third, hit badly, was left smoking. Afterwards the Hurricane pilots thanked the wing for its splendid support and some days later Intelligence reported that all three ships had been sunk.

Ian Gleed wrote up the story of this raid, possibly for his second book (his first was about to be published at this time) which he gave to Teddy Denman and which is reproduced here as it gives a good insight into the way an operation of this type was carried out by his wing.

'It was eleven o'clock and a fine day, the sun was shining from a clear blue sky as I stood by the window of my office sipping my tea. Good day for ops, I thought. As if to answer my thoughts the telephone rang. As I crossed the room to pick it up I somehow knew that this was it.

'"Controller here, sir, I have orders for an operation. Shall I send them up?"

'"No, hang on, I'll come down and get them." I hastily swallowed the last drop of tea, grabbed my scarf from my locker, tore into the Adjutant's office next door, told him I was off to the ops room and would be flying after that. Then quickly out to my car, down the road to the ops room.

'"Morning, old boy, what's the form?" was my greeting to the controller.

'"I've warned the squadrons, sir," he said handing me the typewritten orders.

'"The wing is to escort 8 Hurricane Bombers to the Cherbourg area. Tactics to be at the discretion of the wing leader, who will brief all pilots before take-off. Wing to set course at 14.30 hours. That seems simple. Thank God, it's after lunch, the boys are always in better form with full tummies. I'll brief them at 13.45."

'"OK, sir, I'll let the squadrons know," answered the controller. I went out to the car and drove down to Johnny Carver's office.

'"Morning, sir, what's the form."

'"Good morning, Johnny, did you have a good breakfast, because you'll probably be too frightened to have any lunch. I'll give you the gen. as soon as the others arrive."

'I phoned up the other three squadron commanders and asked them round for a quick conference. Bunny Currant (the 501 CO) arrived first, tall and fair-haired, dressed in a new uniform, the bar of his DFC glinting underneath his wings.

'"Good Heavens, Bunny, where the hell are you going dressed like that? To a mannequin show?"

'"Just my luck," he replied, "I had a date with a new girl friend, the one I met the other night."

'"Bad luck, Bunny, you've had it, there's a show on this afternoon. Good show, here come the other two." They burst into the room, Cam Malfroy, tennis king and CO of 66, the other Pennington-Legh, ex-torpedo dropping king, now CO of the Hurribombers. "Good morning chaps, here's the form." I read them the orders. "66 you be antiflak. I'll be medium cover with you, Bunny. You, Johnny, be rear support. Cam, you and Pennington-Legh have a chat and get your attack organised. Johnny, if you've a good lunch today I'll drive you up to your Mess. See you in the briefing room punctually at 13.45. OK Bunny, OK Cam?"

'"Right, sir, we'll be there." We chatted a bit together, then split up to have a quick lunch.

'Johnny has a very lovely thatched country house as his squadron mess. When we arrived there the pilot boys had already started their lunch. They all knew something was in the air, but as yet they didn't know what. Several humorists asked if it was Berlin this time. They made several cracks at me hoping that I would give them some advanced information. Some of their guesses were very near the mark. At a lunch before a show the boys are usually always very cheerful, though generally don't eat quite as much. I'm afraid that I must admit that the prospect of a show has rather a strange effect on my tummy and I generally leave half my lunch on the plate; most annoying as lunch is generally a very good meal. Contrary to most motion pictures or tales of fighter pilots, the chaps don't drink alcohol before a job of work. They rarely have beer, more often having water or minerals. They have their drinks when they get back at night to celebrate. Even at a party the majority are very moderate drinkers.

'We finish our lunch with a cup of coffee, then hurry out to the lorries and cars that take us down to the briefing room. We trundle down the hill and stop at the long wooden hut on the edge of the 'drome. Already there are several cars and lorries parked outside. This hut is divided into two sections, a small section is the intelligence officer's sanctum, where all the secret gen. is kept, and where all records of combats, special reports, latest information of the enemy, is kept filed and can be seen by the pilots before the show. The other section is a long room filled with chairs, all except one end where there is a raised dais. On the wall are maps and pictures and diagrams of aircraft, ours and the Hun's. Wooden models hang from the ceiling. On the wall at the back of the dais is a large wall map covering the south of England and the northern coast of France.

'There is a hush as I step on to the dais. The room is full with the 42 pilots. On the wall map the intelligence officer has already chalked up our track for today's show. I start the briefing.

'"Good afternoon, chaps. A simple job today, we are to search off Cherbourg and attack any shipping that we see. According to the recce planes there's some there. 66, you are antiflak. As soon as we sight anything, and I give the order to attack, go straight in and keep those Hun gunners' heads down. You Hurribomber boys go in from a slightly different angle, directly on their tails. I'll climb with 501 as soon as I see anything and carry out a feint attack from a different direction, while 118, you look after any Huns that turn up. If a shower arrive we'll give you a hand. Take-off time 14.15, setting course 14.30. Be ready to take synchronised time, it's coming up to 13.53 ... ready ... now. OK, chaps, good luck." Then I give them a few technical instructions about which frequency to use for the operation, and for air sea rescue if anyone gets into trouble. A few other hints then, "OK, chaps, pilots to be in cockpits in seven minutes. Good luck."

'"Now, Bunny, who's my number two?"

'"Flight Sergeant Thomas, sir." OK. On these shows we always work in pairs, so that if anything goes wrong you can look after each other. The boys have streamed out to their planes. After emptying my pockets the IO searches me to make sure that I haven't anything in them that might help the Hun. I too wander out to my plane, put on my Mae West, then climb into the cockpit and check that everything is as it should be. Oxygen OK, maps, compass, gun sight, camera gun switched on ... everything seems all correct. An airman helps me on with my parachute and I make sure that my rubber dinghy is fixed correctly. I relax for a moment and stare round the 'drome; at each aircraft the men are helping their pilots, holding their parachutes for them, polishing the already speckless windscreens. I glance at my watch. Time to start up.

'"All clear?"

'"All clear," comes the reply from the man standing by the starter battery.

'"Contact." I press the starter button and the prop slowly turns over, the engine quickly bursts into life and I start taxiing out to the take off runway. Good show, all the other aircraft have started. I taxi past the Hurribombers, their bombs nearly hidden in the shadows under their wings. I turn on to the runway and wait. The rest of 501 form up in vics of three; one minute to go. I lift my hand, then drop it and slowly open the throttle – we're off.

'We roar low towards the coast, just missing the Church steeples of the little villages. The sky seems very full of aircraft; the Hurribombers with their close escort on my left. As we cross the coast we drop down even lower, skimming just above the waves, a very exhilarating feeling. I settle down to concentrate on the compass. Behind us the English coast soon fades in the haze. Now and then we surprise batches of seagulls; they flash past our cockpits, sometimes making you duck your head because you think they'll hit you. The sea is calm and very blue. About ten miles out it gets very hazy, the visibility getting so low that I can only just see across the formation. I wonder whether to turn back. The Spits are weaving gently keeping a good look out behind. You never know when or where you'll find the Hun. I reconsider my decision whether to turn back, but still carry on.

'At last in front on our right a dark shape looms up, Alderney, most northerly of the Channel Islands. We swing gently left, a few more minutes and the cliffs of Cap de la Hague jump into shape. I break R/T silence by calling quickly, "Turning left," and turn fairly hard. We are too close inshore, there are flashes from the cliffs, behind us are black bursts of flak. Suddenly there are ships ahead. On the R/T I say,

'"Target ahead, go straight in."

'I waggle my wings and opening the throttle start climbing; from a thousand feet I see them clearly, three escort vessels in line abreast formation.

'They have seen us too. Large flashes come from amidships, forward and astern. Black puffs appear unpleasantly close to my right hand aircraft. I am pleased as flashes from all of them show that they are firing at my squadron. As yet they haven't seen the anti-flak squadron tearing in just above the sea, their guns blazing too; little pin pricks of light on the decks and bridge show where their cannon shells are exploding. That should make the gunners duck their heads. Now come the first two Hurricanes, picking a ship each. Blast! The first one has missed – two columns of water jump up from the stern. Oh, good shooting, there is a flash, a heap of debris and smoke, then fire from the centre one. The Hurricanes stream in. Oh, wizard, two direct hits on the stern of the furthest one; simultaneously a very near miss under the bow of the nearest and a direct hit right on the transome.

'A voice on the R/T,

"Hello leader, Johnny here, am with you now," then, "Hell's bells, did you see that, it's blown up." 118 has arrived at the party. That was the centre ship, one moment she was there, flames leaping high with black smoke from amidships, the next moment after a terrific burst of fire she had disappeared, leaving just a few fragments on the water.

'We swung right round, turning over, then it was impossible to see where the last few Hurribombers dropped their eggs because the remaining two ships were enveloped in smoke; one was well on fire and down by the stern, the other stationary with a list to port.

'"OK boys, bloody good, set course for home and weave like hell."

'We turn northwards, the Spits twisting and turning, now's the time for any trouble to start. A glance behind shows both remaining ships in a bad way; the fire on one looks as if it's spread and the other seems to be slowly listing over on to its side; they are both stationary.

'"Ground control calling, enemy aircraft about ten miles south of you."

'"Message received, get a move on, boys."

'The Hurribombers are gradually getting together underneath us, the close escort Spits closing round them. I start counting up the aircraft, six seven … Thank God for that, eight Hurribombers are there. I give up counting the Spits as the haze hides half of them. Anyway, there haven't been any May Day calls on the R/T. I call up ground control and ask them where the Huns are.

'They reply:

'"Not far behind you."

'The weaving Spitfires dart from side to side, the pilots craning their necks searching the sky behind. I judge us to be getting on for half way across. I should love to fly back and have a look at the wreckage now, but I know that is a damned silly thought, because now the place would be a hornet's nest with Messerschmitts buzzing around like flies round a jam pot. At last the white cliffs of England jump into sight in front of us. Soon we see the 'drome, our sweep is over. The squadrons break formation, the aircraft spreading out and hurrying in to land.

'The pilots jump out of their planes and wander along to the briefing room. They are laughing, chatting together, and happy; everyone is back. Two planes have been slightly damaged by bullets. We claim one ship destroyed, one probably destroyed and the third damaged. Everyone slaps each other on the back, "Jolly good show, chaps." We wander out into the sun, ready for another show.'

Over the next few days two things happened which dominated the Gleed household. The first was the publication, on 18 May, of Gleed's own book which he entitled *Arise to Conquer* (Victor Gollancz, 1942), the title derived from 46 Squadron's motto, 'We rise to conquer', the second was the award, four days later, of Gleed's Distinguished Service Order.

Arise to Conquer was a typical product of wartime autobiographies by fighting servicemen, and read by many with much of the same sort of enthusiasm which Gleed had put into it. Naturally being a wartime publication the names used had to be changed, and some of the chronology is slightly awry; when he was writing it he was undoubtedly too busy leading his men in the air to have time to check out all the historical detail that might prove of interest to later readers.

With youthful exuberance he gave copies to his mother, father and sister Daphne, each suitably autographed. They were all delighted with the slim volume and began to read it avidly. However, they very soon began to question one part of it, that being the reference to a certain girlfriend, nay fianceé, by the name of Pam. Who was this girl, they asked, we don't know her? Is she real? Ian smiled sheepishly:

'No of course not but you know what the boys in the squadron are like, they like a touch of romance!' In fact it was at the instigation of his publisher, Victor Gollancz, that Gleed included the female element in the book, to add that little touch of romance. For himself Gleed had no such ties in that direction, firmly believing that as a fighting man in the middle of a war he could allow no such diversions of this sort. There was a branch of W.H. Smith, the booksellers, close to the Gleed home and the manager, quick to seize an opportunity, put on a display for the book in his window – 'local author and hero' stuff was always good for business. However, with so many visitors to the Gleed house, he quickly sold his stock and several times had to quickly re-order copies from the publishers to keep up with the demand.

The award of the Distinguished Service Order was the crowning achievement for Gleed, the fighter pilot and leader. It recognised his prowess as an air fighter and air leader, the citation speaking of his 'fighting spirit' and also of his 'masterly leadership'. It also confirmed the destruction of 12 German aircraft although at this particular moment he had in fact accounted for 15, three being shared. In addition he had probably destroyed seven, including two shared, and damaged at least two others.

Squadron Leader Frank Birchfield engaged a Junkers 88 west of Ibsley on 26 May, being credited with a probable after he had seen strikes on its fuselage and cockpit canopy, followed by a large white flash. On 1 June, Gleed led five squadrons on a sweep and during the afternoon led 501 as top cover to 11 Group's Circus 180, escorting eight Hurribombers on an attack upon an artificial silk factory near Calais. Hornchurch Wing Spitfires acted as cover escort, but again no enemy aircraft were enticed into the air. Two days later Gleed led his wing on a sweep to Cherbourg, escorting Bostons on 10 Group's Circus No 6.

The bombers bombed Cherbourg from 14,000 feet. A Czech squadron flying as high cover was attacked by a large group of FW190s but they shot down one of the attackers. Some 190s made a feint attack on Gleed's formation but did not press it home. On 6 June he led his pilots out again, this time on Ramrod 22 flown by 10 Group.

Pennington-Legh's Hurribombers attacked Maupertus aerodrome yet in the late afternoon. Gleed recorded:

> Bombs dropped on dispersal and perimeter points. Five FWs took off as bombing started. Wing was attacked by 10 as we came out; in the ensuing dogfight one FW was destroyed, one probable and four damaged. Our casualties were two. Portreath rear support wing lost one pilot in a dogfight with FWs.

After the attack, Gleed had led his wing round; 118 Squadron swept as far as Caen but they were attacked by the Focke Wulfs. Johnny Carver (in BL984) and his number two Sergeant L.H. Jones (EN975) went after one 190 but others bounced them. 501 Squadron flying some way off saw the two pilots battling with them very low down near Calvados but unhappily neither of them returned. Carver's was a sad loss to 118 and the wing. He was an ambitious, daring leader, and aggressive fighter pilot, possibly too ambitious for his own safety as it proved. 118 was taken over by E.W. 'Bertie' Wootten DFC of 234 Squadron.

The day following Carver's loss, Gleed had lunch with Group Captain Hardy, Cam Malfroy and Bunny Currant, at Middle Wallop. Group Captain Steven Hardy was the station commander at Wallop and stood 6 feet 7 inches tall, quite a contrast to Gleed's 5 feet 5½ inches. (Gleed weighed 8½ stones – 119 pounds.) Hardy's height made it impossible for him to fly on operations as he could not fit into either a Hurricane or Spitfire with a parachute underneath him, therefore when he did fly he did not carry one. He merely sat in the empty bucket seat when flying either aeroplane around the locality.

Operations continued during June but general activity in the

Ibsley Wing's area decreased slightly. Back with 11 Group on the afternoon of 20 June, a sweep over the Pas de Calais with the Biggin Hill Wing did, however, produce a brief skirmish. The whole show was a diversion for bombers attacking Le Havre and Gleed's wing suffered for a failure in communication. Several enemy fighters were seen sniffing about and a dozen Messerschmitt 109s were driven off. Then three vics of FW190s dived upon 501 Squadron and Flight Sergeant V. Bauman, a Czech pilot, went down (AB497) and was reported missing. Gleed's comments on this action were:

> Crossed coast by Hardelot. Swept to St Omer and acted as a diversion to the bombing of Le Havre. (120 FWs in this area but the controller forgot to mention it!!!) We saw about 45 of them. 501 were split up in a dogfight and we were attacked all the way out. Casualties were five.

Pilot Officer J.A. Jackson got in a burst at one of the attackers which went down in a spiral dive trailing smoke. Four days later Bunny Currant received a well earned DSO and was then rested, his squadron being taken over by yet another Battle of Britain veteran Squadron Leader J.W. Villa DFC and bar, known inevitably as 'Pancho'.

Yet another show took place on 26 June:

> Led wing as target support wing for bombers on Le Havre. Crossed coast at Fecamp and orbited Le Havre. Bombers left target underneath us. We were attacked by six FW190s who ran away when we turned to meet them. Two of our aircraft were damaged.

Gleed and Currant again lunched at Middle Wallop with Group Captain Hardy on the 30th. They were joined by Supermarine's Chief Test Pilot Geoffrey Quill, Squadron Leader Blackadder and Wing Commander E.H. Thomas, OC of the Biggin Hill Wing. Geoffrey Quill's name has now become synonomous with that of the Spitfire, for he had done much of the testing of this famous aeroplane before and during the war. During the Battle of Britain he had managed to get himself attached to 65 Squadron to evaluate

16. *(Top)* Widge in a serious mood, seated in his Spitfire (probably AB380). Wing Commander's penant by windscreen and Figaro painted on light blue background.

17. *(Bottom)* Boxing Day 1942. Ian Gleed with his mother and sister Daphne. This was the last time the family was together for he flew to North Africa three days later.

18. *(Left)* Spitfire Vb (ER170). A new Figaro flown by Wing Commander Gleed in North Africa February 1943.

21. *(Right)* Squadron Leader Peter Olver DFC, Gleed's right hand man in 244 Wing, DAF 1943.

22. *(Far right)* Flight Lieutenant John Stuart Taylor (later Squadron Leader DFC & bar), one of Gleed's particular friends in North Africa. He flew with 145 Squadron before commanding 601. He died trying to land his damaged Spitfire on July 12, 1943.

23. *(Right)* Widge and Figaro (AB502) flying over the Tunisian Coast.

19. *(Left)* Gleed's groundcrew painting his initials and Figaro on ER170

20. *(Left)* Desert Air Force Figaro on ER170. In the desert, a palm tree was added to the insignia.

24. AB502 at readiness; trolley-acc plugged in, all ready to scramble!

25. Close up of Figaro on AB502, Gleed's last Spitfire. This painted mascot was salvaged from the crashed machine and returned to Gleed's family.

26. Three successful fighter pilots in Gleed's 244 Wing. l to r : Flight Lieutenant D F 'Jerry' Westrana (later Squadron Leader DFC & bar), Flying Officer Neville Duke DFC (later Squadron Leader DSO OBE DFC & 2 bars AFC), and flight Lieutenant P H 'Hunk' Humphreys (later Squadron Leader DFC).

the Spitfire in combat. He did well and shot down several German aircraft. He and Ronnie Harker, Chief Test Pilot for Hawkers, often visited the squadrons to see how things were developing in the air war and occasionally flew on operations with the wing.

After lunch the group went for a swim, Bunny Currant remembers the scene vividly:

The huge towering figure of Group Captain Hardy standing on the edge of the pool, alongside him laughing (as always) the minute figure of Widge. Both hurling themselves into the water to scrap for the yellow pilot's dinghy floating on the surface. Hardy had a very quiet manner and a modest sense of humour. Widge was a bubbling, infectious, bouncing fellow; such a contrast to each other.

Sad to relate, Hardy was to die a short while afterwards following a severe attack of hiccoughs.

Ian Gleed had now flown over 40 missions as wing leader and his last operation with his wing occurred on 15 July, 1942. Flying with long range fuel tanks they flew over the Cherbourg peninsula early that morning in company with Malfroy's squadron, with 118 and 501 acting as top cover. Two FW190s were bounced by 66 Squadron who shot down one of them and damaged the second. Gleed's own words for his last operation at the head of the Ibsley Wing were:

Used long range jettisonable tanks for the first time ever. Led 118 Squadron. Set course from base at 0845. Crossed Needles Angels 10 climbing to point half way between Le Havre and Barfleur. The Wing jettisoned its tanks and crossed the tip of Cherbourg peninsula going NW. Patrolled between Cap de Le Havre and Barfleur. Two FW190s seen and jumped by 66 Squadron at Angels 26. One destroyed and one damaged. Our Casualties nil. Final sweep for some time.

Gleed's last sortie was flown the same day as another famous fighter pilot and wing leader made his last flight. This was Wing Commander Brendan 'Paddy' Finucane DSO DFC and two bars who was leader of the Hornchurch Wing. Leading his squadrons in an attack against an enemy troop encampment at low level near Etaples, south of Boulogne, he was hit in the radiator by a machine gunner on the coastal sand dunes on his way in. After the attack he was forced to ditch in the Channel. His Spitfire hit the water and went straight under taking Finucane with it.

Gleed's position as wing leader of the Ibsley Wing went to Wing Commander P. Gibbs. One can only wonder at what Gleed might have achieved had he remained on operations for a few more weeks and been with his wing during the Dieppe Raid which took place on 19 August. On that occasion Gibbs led all three squadrons several times during that great air battle above the beaches and towns of Dieppe and the wing, including Gibbs, made several claims.

However, Gleed was sent to Fighter Command Headquarters as Wing Commander Tactics with effect from 16 July. Stationed once again near London, he was able to visit his family more frequently but rather than stay there he rented Beverley Nichols' house at 1 Ellerdale Close, Hampstead. Here he was free from the restrictions which his mother may have imposed when the energetic Gleed went the round of the many parties, dances or shows to which he was invited. He knew his mother would insist that he rest as much as possible following his tiring flying tour.

On the second anniversary of 15 September, 1940, which was being called Battle of Britain day, Gleed was among those pilots who were invited to attend a reunion and service to commemorate the anniversary. Air Chief Marshal Sir Hugh Dowding who had led Fighter Command during the battle met the men, many of whom had become household names over the country. Al Deere, Sailor Malan, Tony Bartley, Desmond Sheen, Max Aitken, Johnny Kent, Brian Kingcome, Richard Hillary, Douglas Watkins, R.H. Gretton, plus one WAAF officer, Elspeth Henderson MM. Dowding said of these officers:

I am proud and happy to be surrounded by these pilots, two years older, with more rings on their sleeves and more ribbons on their chests. If they had what they deserved their chests and sleeves would be completely obliterated with embroidery.

One pleasant duty he had to perform during this rest period was his second visit to Buckingham Palace to receive his DSO. Once again the small, proud figure of Ian Gleed stood before his King as His Majesty hooked the medal, probably one of the most beautiful and attractive decorations, on his left breast under his RAF pilot wings.

In December he changed his job and title to Wing Commander Operations at Fighter Command HQ. This second 'chairborne' job did not last long for with the war in North Africa gaining victorious momentum air leaders were required in that theatre. Gleed volunteered and once again his experience and flair were needed.

He spent his last Christmas with his family at Finchley. On Boxing Day they took photographs of each other. It was to be the last time they would be together; the two doctors, the mother and the fighter pilot. Later he dined with his friend Teddy Denman before leaving to take a quick conversion course onto the Vickers Wellington in which he would fly to North Africa via Gibraltar. Teddy Denman remembers that Gleed was tremendously excited at the prospect of flying in the desert and eager to be off.

Wing Commander I.R. Gleed DSO DFC was posted to Headquarters, RAF Middle East with effect from 1 January, 1943.

CHAPTER ELEVEN

The trip to North Africa

Wing Commander Ian Gleed was preparing his second book. Already ideas were formulating and as we have seen in the previous chapter he had already put down some of his thoughts. When he flew to North Africa, he stopped over at Gibraltar, and while staying at the Rock Hotel, typed out a draft covering the flight out, completing it at Darragh North, Beni Ulid in a howling sandstorm on 12 February, 1943. His death prevented any further writing and of course his second book did not see the light of day. It is, therefore, perhaps fitting to include his writings in this story of his life. Here then, in his own words, is the account of his journey to the war in North Africa.

'At last Q for Queenie was all set to go. The weather forecasts were good, so we planned to fly to the forward aerodrome the next day. The weather expert proved right. The sun was shining as we walked to the hangar after breakfast.

'I borrowed the Ferry Flight CO's car and returned to the mess. John and I filled it with our luggage, then back to the hangars where everything had to be weighed. The total amount allowed was 230 pounds. That was counting your own weight, flying clothes and everything else.

'I knew that I was well within the limits as I only weigh $8\frac{1}{4}$ stone, but John, although he didn't look it, weighed $14\frac{1}{2}$ stone which didn't leave much over for luggage. Anyway we wangled through the weighing, and drove the baggage out to the plane and started stowing it. We shoved about nine kit bags in the bomb bays and lashed the others in the aircraft, putting John's and my luggage in the front turret position, the front turret being removed on the torpedo carrier to save weight. Our ulterior motive for putting it there was that it would be the last lot to be thrown overboard if we got into trouble and wanted to lighten the plane. Then a few quick farewells and thanks to the CO and to Sandy who had taught me to fly Wimpeys, and we were off.

'John took off and I landed as I knew the forward 'drome that we were bound for well. We were soon airborne and on our way. The first thing that went wrong was George; the automatic pilot didn't work. Now George on a long trip is almost indispensable as it's very hard work flying a heavy bomber, particularly in bumpy weather. We went on hoping that a George expert would be at the forward 'drome.

'After an hour and a half we changed position, a procedure that can be carried out with perfect comfort and safety if the automatic pilot is flying the machine. As it wasn't, it made things difficult. I descended to the bomb aimer's floor, whilst John, having trimmed the plane to fly straight and level, slipped out of the seat. I immediately jumped up to slip into the seat; unfortunately my parachute harness caught in some projection behind me and just prevented me from reaching the control. At the same time I was blocking the gangway and quite immobile, thus preventing John from reaching the controls as well. In the meantime, Q for Queenie had started a dive, which appeared to be steepening. I tugged to pull myself free whilst John tried to untangle me at the back. I came free with a jerk and pulled the control column back and all went well. The crew were not amused.

'We arrived eventually, after dodging some very nasty looking rain clouds, at our destination. We circled the 'drome which is perched on top of cliffs looking onto the sea, and lowered the undercarriage. The wheels came down but all the green lights on the dashboard that tell the pilot that the wheels are locked down, did not. We peered out of the window. They looked OK; I throttled right back to see if the warning hooter blew; it didn't so we thought the wheels must be locked. To make sure, John pumped the emergency lever.

'We landed and all was well, the undercarriage did not collapse, but the starboard wheel's green lights were still on. We found that we were meant to be leaving that night, but the dispatching officer would not let us go as he thought the wheels might collapse and wanted to make quite sure. So we resigned ourselves to a boring wait, had a few drinks, played draughts, read a bit and went to bed.

'The next morning we checked our machine, chased up the ground crews who eventually fixed the green light; the undercarriage had been in no danger of collapsing. We were briefed at 5 o'clock, told exactly what tracks to fly on, how to land at Gibraltar etc. We were shown photographs of Cap Finisterre which would be our landfall after crossing the Bay of Biscay, photographs of Gibraltar and we were told the procedure of landing there. We were to leave at 04.30 the following morning and would be called at 1.30 and could have breakfast at 2.00. We pushed off to bed at 9 o'clock after an early supper. Neither of us could sleep so we talked and I found out a bit about my co-pilot John.

'By profession he was a policeman. After nine years he had become a station inspector and his job was waiting for him after the war. He had been in London during the great blitzes and on his own admission joined the RAF because he was fed up with being bombed. He has seen such hideous sights that the one thing he didn't want to become was a bomber pilot. He was married and had a daughter aged four and was expecting a son at any moment. He was twenty-nine, three years older than me.

'After chatting about this and that we dropped asleep. A batman woke us. The wind was howling round the eaves of the little Devon cottage that was our billet and the rain was pelting down. Not a hopeful awakening. We dressed quickly and staggered through a driving rain to the bus that took us to the mess where we had an excellent breakfast of bacon and egg, a luxurious meal that improved our tempers. Then out to the briefing room to be told that the weather was hopeless and the trip was cancelled. We cursed and staggered back to bed. We slept till lunchtime, checked up on Q for Queenie, played a few games of draughts, worried the Met man, who prophesied good weather for the following morning, then to bed. The batman woke us and once more the wind screamed and rain beat our faces as we staggered to the bus. Once more we ate an excellent egg and bacon breakfast, then down to the briefing room to find what the weather experts had to say. The forecaster was convinced that the weather would be fine the other end, so if we could get through 6,000 feet of cloud after take off we would be in clear weather all the way; the clouds would probably start breaking when we reached the Spanish coast line. So off we decided to go.

'"Spike," the rear gunner, collected the thermos flasks filled with coffee and the packages of food. "Mac", the navigator, checked his courses and we planned our flight plan. First climb through cloud and stay high until the clouds broke, then descend and map read our way round the coast. I left it to John to take off as I had never flown a Wimpey at night.

'It was drizzling as we clambered into the plane, the wind buffeting us and gently rocking the Wimpey as we climbed the ladder. It was a miserable farewell to England. I found that I was far too engrossed in the prospect of the flight to even remember that I was stepping off English soil for the last time for some months, perhaps years.

'The cockpit lights, an orange/red, glowed warmly; we seemed to be in a world of our own, outside the rain beat on the windscreen. John sat confidently at the controls, I stood feeling rather windy at his side. I had heard some unpleasant stories of Wimpeys crashing on take off when heavily loaded. The crew took up their positions, after running up the engines and testing the mags. we waved the chocks away and taxied out. On the 'drome the flare path lay, glim lights dotting the ground like fallen stars. A green Aldis light winked our letter from the end of the lights and we were off. John opened the throttles, letting the brakes off when we were half throttle, the heavy machine lumbered forward, lights flashed past us. I stared at the airspeed indicator, 40 mph, 50, 55, 60, the speed slowly crept up. The darkness beyond the end flares seemed to be rushing at us like a wall, 80 mph, now. John jerked the stick back and she left the ground. Wheels up first at 1,000 feet, up with the flaps, we had used 10° to help us come unstuck. Then we were in the cloud, I knew at once because our navigation lights suddenly shone back from the wing tips, a bright green circle of light from the starboard wing, a duller red one from the port. We climbed slowly, I glanced at John's face, he still looked very confident, staring at the instrument panel. The altimeter needle crawled slowly round; we were climbing at 350 feet per minute, my normal climb in a Spitfire is 3,000 feet per minute. Up, slowly, stolidly, steadily we clambered for height. I felt glad that John was flying, at this rate it would be twenty minutes before we were above the clouds. I stared but could see no sign of stars. Out of the side window I could see the engine, the circular exhausts glowing bright

red. We steadied onto our compass course, still climbing; it was
5.20 am, the first day of 1943.

'Slowly, steadily the altimeter needle crawled round, to me it
seemed years, standing by John, staring into nothingness, the
cockpit clock seemed to have stopped. Invisible beneath the cloud
England slid astern. I knew that part of the coast well. At last a star
glimmered feebly through the blackness, only to disappear again.
Twenty minutes after take off we were in the clear starlit sky, just
skimming the cloud tops at 8,000 feet.

'Mac the navigator gave us a change of course, that meant that
we were just passing over the Scilly Isles. Above the clouds it was
easy flying, a sliver of waning moon lit the sky. After an hour and a
half I took over; this time we managed to change places without
mishap, George, the automatic pilot, flew the plane smoothly and
accurately, much more so than a human pilot could. In the driver's
seat all one had to do was to lean back, keep an eye on the compass
to see that we didn't wander from our course, and check up that all
instruments were reading normal.

'So at last I had left England. Had I been wise to volunteer to do
operations in the Middle East, time would tell. I was thrilled at the
adventure of flying but, my chief worry was that the engines would
pack up and drop us all in the Bay of Biscay. We should be very
unlucky if that happened as the trip and many longer ones had
been done many thousand times by sturdy Wellingtons. We
wandered on smoothly cruising at 117 knots; it seemed absurdly
slow to my fighter boy mind.

'There was nothing to do and nothing happened for the next
hour and a half. John and I changed over. Just as we were
changing, the undercarriage red lights, that shine when the
undercarriage is locked up and show green when it's locked down,
went out. We then made a mistake. I told John to put the
undercarriage selector lever to wheels up. He did. All that
happened was the wheels fell out; all our hydraulic oil had leaked
away. We were three quarters of the way across the Bay of Biscay
with both wheels hanging out, bad weather behind, and no flaps to
use when we landed which meant a fast approach and touch down.
Still it was no use worrying about that until we arrived at Gib. We
were still fairly heavily loaded, and with the extra drag caused by
the wheels hanging down she would just keep 100 knots and

No lights when u/c is locked up.

maintain height at maximum economical cruising. If we went any faster it meant that we were burning much too much petrol. As it was our petrol consumption was about 25 gallons per hour more than it should be – we discovered that after the first hour. Some quick calculation showed that we would have enough to get to Gib, but not too much to spare.

'The red glow on the engine cowlings grew brighter and the engine temperatures rose, the port engine getting much higher than the starboard one – it sounded rough. The whole plane seemed to be vibrating. For a while we flew in silence, then John suggested throttling back a bit to cool down the engines. I pulled the revs down a bit and throttled back; we began to sink, losing about 50 feet per minute. John then suggested flying slower but this wouldn't do as I knew the engines would get hotter still. I kept the revs down and opened the throttle a bit, although we were flying at a greater throttle opening than the weak mixture setting we tried the weak mixture lever in weak position. We throbbed steadily on.

'The sky in the east grew lighter, first a faint yellow streak just above the horizon then it spread, the stars growing dimmer and eventually becoming invisible. Below us clouds showed up looking like a rough carpet of grey dirty cotton wool. Mac the navigator told us we should see the coastline of Spain in half an hour. I felt relieved. The engines sounded very uneven and it was a surprise to me that they kept running, the temperatures were high, the port engine staying a few degrees below maximum emergency; five minutes flying as the Manual put it.

'It grew lighter quickly, soon instead of seeing a grey shadow the camouflage colours showed on the wings. If the engines stopped now at least we would be able to do a reasonable crash landing. Mac crawled down into the bomb aimer's position in the nose with a map. It was the rear gunner who sighted land first, in his broad Scot voice he said, 'We just passed over some rocks.' We were only ten minutes late in making landfall. I guessed that we had a stronger wind behind us than we had allowed for. Now we could land in sunny Spain, burn our plane and have a holiday while we walked to Gib or Lisbon. I felt happier and in a way rather hoped that the engines would stop. I had utmost confidence that we could force lob safely and would escape.

'John and I changed positions again. Mac suggested that we

should fly beneath the clouds and map read, following the coast around. We dived fast, so fast that the dangling wheels blew back up and the engine temperatures sank to normal cruising heat. We flew about seven miles off the coast. On the mainland the mountains were blue shapes in the background of green fields and white houses. Then the wheels fell out again.

'The worst part of the journey was over. The atmosphere in the plane felt more relaxed. We opened our packets of food and drank some coffee. The food was disappointing, biscuits, when I had hoped to find meat sandwiches, and several sorts of chocolate bars and packets of raisins. The coffee tasted good and refreshed us. By now I was getting used to the throb of the rough port engine but the temperatures showed no inclination to rise. Back home my parents would just be sitting down for breakfast. I felt homesick.

'Now and then we changed course slightly to avoid small coastal steamers and fleets of small fishing craft. The clouds were dispersing, the water grew an even deeper blue. We approached Lisbon and flew closer inshore to have a look. The view was very beautiful, bright yellow beaches with small highly coloured houses and villas facing the sea, round the bend of the river the town itself, looking clean and alive in the distance. Soon we were past, the coast gradually slipped out of sight, the land becoming just a blue shadow on the horizon.

'Time passed. I started getting in a bit of a flap about the petrol, as our consumption was very high. We throttled down a bit; Q for Queenie was flying more easily as she was getting much lighter as we had used about 500 gallons of petrol so far. I studied the map and decided that we should cut across Cape St Vincent, the southern tip of Portugal. If we used our reserve tanks, we should be all right but that was cutting it a bit fine. The port engine still ran rough and it would have been no surprise to me if it had stopped suddenly.

'I began to get tired. I was so bored that I would have welcomed something exciting happening, like a forced landing. Suddenly Spike, the rear gunner called up.

'"Skipper, there's a plane between us and the mainland, on the port beam."

'John at the controls opened the throttles and climbed for the clouds. I caught a fleeting glimpse of a plane but then lost it in the clouds. I took over the controls. We were approaching Cape St

Vincent, so we swung inland, crossing over a yellow beach, a high cliff then over rough mountainous country. The landscape was like a toy world perfectly coloured. Above a dome of blue, to the south the sea was that almost unbelievable blue that you see on post cards sent from the south of France. We flew over a village and the people stopped in the street and stared upwards. So this was Portugal, a peaceful happy looking countryside.

'We crossed out over the coast before we reached the Spanish border. Spain looked as lovely as Portugal. There was no sign of the terrific internal struggle that had been the practice ground for this war. Oh, England, if only you had sent but one squadron of Hawker Furys to fight in Spain the warring Axis might have got a bit of RAF justice and thought again before plunging into war.

'Our journey was nearly over, to the south mountains of Africa rose on the horizon. Soon we passed Cadiz, then Cap Trafalgar where England once before showed that she was anything but a second rate power. The flight engineer stood ready to turn on to the reserve tanks. I had a drink of coffee and felt refreshed. The last few miles before we could see the Rock of Gibraltar seemed to take an age. Then we were round the bend of the coast and there it was. My first impression was that it was much smaller than I expected. It gave me an odd thrill to see several large ships including aircraft carriers in the harbour. Across the bay, Algeçiras, a cluster of houses and hotels glistened in the sun. We circled the Rock, it grew in immensity as we closed, massive concreted sides loomed above us as we flew low to look at the 'drome. What a 'drome! A wide streak of concrete built on the flat neck joining the Rock to the mainland, lined with an assortment of aircraft on either side. It looked absurdly small. Still land we must, we had not enough petrol to go to Algiers or any other 'drome.

'Mac and I started arguing which way the wind was blowing. He should know as he had been checking it from time to time. I thought it was blowing the other way as I could see some small boats swinging at anchor. We pumped the wheels down using the emergency bottle, tried to put the flaps down, but as we expected, they didn't move. Just as we were turning in for a practice approach I saw a plane coming in to land the other way. Mac was wrong – I opened the engines wide and swung round, heading for Africa, gave the Rock a wide berth, flew right round and settled down on the approach the other way. The 'drome still looked impossibly small, the one runway when seen on end seemed about the size of a matchbox, the sea at either end. If we overshot we would fall straight in the harbour. I had heard quite a few stories of this happening. Pleasant thoughts!

'I had the utmost confidence that I could land Queenie safely. I put the airscrew control into fully fine, the revs. rose and the engines bellowed. We straightened up and I steadied the speed at 90 knots. The end of the runway was right on the sea. I knew that if we were to stop in time I should have to touch down right on this edge.

'It stared beneath us, but the sea gave us no idea how high we were, on the other side of the 'drome there were boats in the harbour, but this side there was just blue sea. The sun reflected off its smooth surface like a glass. We floated lower, I was aiming at the edge of the runway. This is OK, I'll do it nicely. The aircraft lined up on either side of the runway which rushed up towards me, there would be no room for a swing. I pulled the nose up a little and closed the throttle. Queenie hit the deck with a bump, bounced, hit again and stayed down, developed a bad swing to the left, we missed a Liberator parked on the edge by inches, using full brakes we stopped. There were cries from the back.

'"The tail wheel's on fire."

'Clouds of dust flooded the cockpit. John seized the fire extinguisher and jumped out. I switched the engines off and followed rapidly. Poor Queenie's tail wheel wasn't on fire, it was knocked up into the tail end, and the remnants were acting as a tail skid. I now realised how we had stopped so suddenly. Our downfall had been the edge of the runway which was built up forming a sea wall. I had cut it too fine to the extent of three inches and just caught the tail wheel on it. It wasn't a very happy arrival but at least we had arrived in one piece. Poor John was quite convinced that he could have done it much better. I wasn't.

'We were in luck's way. Another Wellington which had had its wheels retracted by mistake about three weeks before was ready for testing. We could take that thus saving time whilst waiting for Queenie to be repaired. Our flying time from England was eight hours. We took all our kit out of the aircraft, piled it in a lorry and went to lunch.

'Gibraltar time is an hour ahead of English time. Although the bar was shut I persuaded the waiter to open it and bring us two large sherries. I wouldn't have been so insistent if I had realised then that it was 3 o'clock not 2 o'clock as I imagined. Delicious sherry at 7d per glass improved our tempers.

'The aerodrome at Gibraltar is a fine engineering achievement; it is built on the old racecourse and the runway is double the width of a normal English one. The town I had always visualised as lying on the sea side of the rock; it doesn't – it nestles under the Rock on the Spanish side. The main Spanish road runs across the 'drome. Policemen hold up the traffic whilst aircraft take off and land. The Spanish border is only a few hundred yards from the edge of the runway. Sometimes aircraft fly over Spain when they circle the 'drome. The Spanish AA gunners were in the habit of opening fire on them. Just before I landed the gunners had opened up on a Spitfire; one of our soldiers saw the gun crew working their gun just across the border, so opened up on them with a Tommy gun, they were only 300 yards away. He wiped them all out, was immediately arrested and removed to jail. Since then the Spanish gunners have been silent and don't notice the aircraft flying low over their heads.

'My billet was to be the Rock Hotel. A large staff car arrived to take me there; in it were Johnny and Barry. They had arrived a week before, but bad weather over the Sahara desert had held them up. They were browned off with Gib and hoping to leave that night.

'I asked John to dinner, then drove to the Hotel, a fairly new modern building built half way up the Rock overlooking the harbour and Spain beyond. The rooms were small but pleasant. Hot and cold water and very comfortable beds. I had some tea then had a bath and felt better, much better. John met me in the bar where we had some more sherry, the most perfect dry sherry I had ever tasted, 1/4d a glass. We had many sherries, beer at 2/6d a bottle at dinner, which was soup (a vague kind), fish with a thick white sauce, roast beef and fruit for dessert. Oranges, tangerines, bananas and nuts. A very smooth port with our coffee, then to bed. John was billeted at the transit camp on the 'drome. He walked home. I stared out of my window at the many lights. There was no black-out because all the Spanish towns kept their lights on and the worst navigator in the world could find Gibraltar by pin-pointing the Spanish towns. Big centrally hung lamps lit the streets of

Gibraltar, while lights shone from windows of the houses, some dull, some coloured shining through their curtains others bright through open windows. It was a beautiful sight that gave me strange pangs of happy memories of days of peace.

'I rose late, 9.30 breakfast. Then drove down to the 'drome to see what the new plane was like. It was K for Katie and was still in bits and wouldn't be ready for testing until after lunch. I wandered along to the briefing room where I learnt that we were meant to be leaving that night. I soon fixed that, for I was not going to leave until we had given K for Katie a good test and I was not going to do ten hours' night flight on top of a lengthy test. They were very pleasant about it and left it to me.

'We lunched at the 'drome after a walk in the town. We both sent cables to England from the post office. The shops in the town were open until one o'clock then they closed until 4 o'clock for a siesta. John and I bought ourselves oranges and tangerines, 2½d each. The shops were mostly filled with curiosities offered for sale at high prices. A finely carved line of elephants, Father, the large one, leading the young with a tiny elephant at the back was offered at £5. Silk kimonos were offered at the same price.

'After lunch we took K for Katie for a test flight, climbing high over the Mediterranean, to the north the mountains of Spain, snow capped shone in the sun. The African mountains loomed blue in the south. The engines ran smoothly, the controls although stiff were safe, but George did not work. We dived and swung into land safely.

'It was a hot sunny day, we were glad to reach the hotel and sip drinks on the verandah outside overlooking the harbour. It seemed very peaceful and far from the war, yet men in uniform and fighting ships and aircraft were all visible at a glance. To me England seemed only a hundred miles or so round the Spanish coast, a normal flight would be seven hours. What a colossal difference air travel makes to travelling time. If only after this war, the people of this mad world travel enough by air, see how each of us lives, we may lose some of the selfishness that is the cause of war.

'Two pilots walked up, it was the Ogre and Milch, sergeant pilots from my old squadron, now pilot officers. The squadron were still flying Hurricanes and were hoping to have a good crack at the Hun in Tunisia. We drank together and talked of old times. We had wine for dinner and of course the usual sherry and port.

'As I walked rather dimly into breakfast a voice I knew well called me. John Simpson, now with four stripes on his arm, he was a Group Captain Operations at Algiers. Last time I had seen him he was a wing commander at combined headquarters in London. He was at Gib trying to get hold of some Spitfire IXs to cope with the FW190s. The Hun had carried out a big raid on a convoy just as it was entering the harbour, 60 Stukas escorted by 80 FW190s. Four squadron of Spit. Vs had intercepted. They knocked down 12 FW190s, lost 10, two of our pilots being safe. They never got near the Stukas. Some of the 190s had carried bombs. One had rolled onto its back at 10,000 feet, dived vertically at a large tanker, failed to pull out and crashed into it with its bomb still on. The tanker was still burning four days later. John Simpson dashed off to do lots of work. I lay in an armchair on the verandah and basked in the sun. I wrote some of this manuscript, scrambled through several very old books, had tea, then a bath and I was all set to go.

'The car failed to arrive and after some frantic telephoning we were told the weather was bad and our departure would be delayed. We were not at all amused. We decided that we would try somewhere in town for dinner. The streets were crowded as usual and we could hear a mixture of music, the feminine dance bands were at it hammer and tongs. When I got back to the hotel I met one of the RAF officers who I knew by sight but whose name I never could remember. He told me that the guns were going to carry out firing practice when a practice alarm went sometime between 10 and 12 pm; would I like to come and watch? I most certainly would.

'We set off with a couple of navy types in a staff car following a track that led us above the town. Sentries halted us several times, the third time they told us we would have to park our car and walk.

'We were about two thirds of the way up the rock, soldiers were lining the path. We found a concrete balustrade and sat on it. A small boat was fussing around the floating targets clearly visible by its navigation lights. Searchlights shining from holes all over the face of the rock swept out to sea. A friendly major explained what was about to happen. This was a pretended invasion of Gib. At zero hour the searchlights would sweep, pick up the targets, then the guns had three minutes to fire as much ammunition as possible.

'Suddenly, with a crack and a splutter, a green Very light soared up from just below us. Guns fired, beams of searchlights leapt into the sky. Above an intense anti-aircraft barrage filled the sky with man made bursting comets. Below, streaking towards the targets clearly illuminated with pom-pom shells, yellow, green, red and white, seemingly bouncing across the water like some giant bead necklace being flung away. On and around the targets bursts of fire and smoke, columns of water, showing where the heavier gun's missiles were falling. It was good shooting. The noise was deafening, a machine gun nest was firing somewhere just behind us, above the stutter of its fire, the bullets cracked as they whistled past my left ear. Then a red Very light soared up and at once there was silence. The searchlights doused one by one and the show was over. As a demonstration of modern fire power it left no doubt in my mind that any invading force viewing the fireworks from the other end of the barrels would be knocked sky high.

'The following day, apart from a walk into the town to buy some soap, I did nothing. I sat and rested hoping very hard that we should definitely start that night. The staff car arrived and I piled in my luggage and we sped through the town to the 'drome. The crew were ready, piling their luggage into K for Katie, we were all very happy to be on the move again. At briefing we stared hard at many photographs. Mac checked and re-checked the tracks and courses. Spike and Sammy collected the rations, far better ones this time, oranges, meat sandwiches, bars of chocolate, cheese wrapped in silver paper and of course coffee.

'Our route was not direct, we were dodging as much as possible flying over enemy territory, although there probably weren't any night fighters, we didn't want to be shot down by flak. So our route took us many miles across the Sahara desert. The Met forecast was not too good. We were told that there were clouds covering the North African mountains, reaching 9,000 feet. In these clouds were heavy icing conditions. Our flight plan was to climb above these and cruise at 10,000 feet. I knew that we wouldn't get her much higher than that for some hours after take off as with her overload tanks full Katie was no light weight. We received final take-off instructions from the control tower. We were to be first off. I tried not to remember all the nasty stories of Wellington crashes.

'We helped each other into our parachute harnesses. The crew clambered in one by one. Turned on the interior lighting, tested the inter-com – first snag, it didn't work. We hastily agreed that we would go without it, the wireless op. started rapidly taking many bits to pieces. John had said at briefing:

'"If the engines pack up, sir, we bale out, I suppose?"'

'"Yes, John, we do," I replied, "Junior, you had better take the water container with you, that's obviously the flight engineer's job." We would have to bale out as landing on mountains on a dark night had only one ending. I imagine flinging myself out through the escape hatch. After a bale out it would be quite likely that we would land miles apart and not meet again. Unpleasant thoughts. It's strange how confident I feel that I shall survive this war. As I clambered up the ladder into Katie I felt quite certain that I should step out in 10 hours' time on African soil.

'John started the engines, ran them up and taxied out. A green light flashed from the control tower. The engines bellowed full power, a hiss of escaping air as John released the brakes. We lumbered forward, the light of the flare path seemingly gradually gaining speed flashing past the cockpit windows. We were almost upon the red lights at the end of the runway when John jerked the stick back. We seem to hang in the air. Wheels up quickly. I wondered if we would miss all the masts of ships in the harbour. The altimeter barely crawled round, we seemed perpetually stuck at 150 feet. Very gingerly we banked into a left hand turn, lights of a Spanish town seemed very near, behind those lights were mountains, the dark mass that was the Rock stood sharply outlined against the stars, the lights of this flare path like a corridor carpet at its base.

'We climbed laboriously, it took five minutes to reach 1,000 feet. The engines throbbed smoothly. The inter-com suddenly came to life; good show on the wireless operator's part. The lights of Gibraltar and Spain faded behind us, below the Mediterranean, a warmer spot to drop in than the Atlantic. I don't know why I kept thinking of dropping into the drink, the sea always rather frightens me when I am flying over it, the engine always sounds rough and most people get this 'enginitus'.

'Then I took over, about five minutes later we ran into cloud. I could see it coming, stars being blacked out by a bank of cloud towering above. As we entered it complete darkness enveloped us like a blanket. The luminous instruments and the soft dashboard lights gleamed softly. Already the windscreen changed from a black square to an indistinct grey – ice was forming quickly on the outside. I was sweating, pushing and pulling at the controls, the only thing to do was to climb. Now and then sharp cracks and knocks sounded by our sides, ice was being flung off the airscrews and was hitting our fuselage like bullets. I found that I had dropped a couple of hundred feet and sweated even more. I could feel the sweat running down my legs; below us were the Atlas mountains, their tops covered in cloud. We must get above this cloud.

'"I can see a star," said John over the intercom. Looking out sideways through the open cockpit window I could see several stars, also the rough mountainous cloud tops. In front I could see nothing so was still on instruments. The windscreen was covered with a layer of thick ice. John started pumping the de-icer, after much sweating on his part about half the ice dropped off.

'After a while we seemed to be fairly securely above the clouds so I put George in; to my relief it worked well, all I had to do was sit back whilst the stick wobbled around controlled by George. Now and then I twiddled either one or other of the two knobs that control the direction and height.

'Now below us we could see the mountains, rearing their ugly rugged tops, around them was the Sahara Desert. After the clouds it was interesting staring downwards. The desert seemed pin pricked with lights, Arab fires, for we were too far south for any Huns. As the hours slipped by we came to the salt lakes, stretching for miles beneath us, glinting and showing up clearly beneath us. Soon we should be passing Sfax then out to sea. When I took over again I turned George out. George when flying a plane is the answer to a gunner's prayer. As we approached the coast I took anti-flak precautions, turning, diving and climbing, it would put off any night fighters that were after us too. Nothing disturbed our peace of mind, no flak, no night fighters and the dark mass of land slid beneath us to be replaced by the sea. Malta somewhere out of sight to the north, Tripoli full of Huns and Italians invisible to the south.

'Mac and I started an argument over the intercom on what the real time was. We were navigating on GMT and had our watches set at Gib time. What I wanted to know was what time we could expect dawn. As we agreed I saw the first sign, a false dawn, a pale pink strip of sky just peeped over the horizon, then it faded into nothingness. Suddenly colour showed, first a faint pink, then yellow, changing to orange red; a pale blue as delicate as a flower grew over the sky above us, the darkness was turning into a deep blue.

'I munched a sandwich, drank some coffee and thought that life was very good. A couple more hours and, God willing, we would be landing safely in Africa.'

CHAPTER TWELVE

Wing Leader – Desert Air Force

Ian Gleed was eager to take up his new appointment, yet even he was the first to appreciate that it would take time for him to assimilate his new surroundings and to understand the nature of operations in this theatre. Although an experienced fighter pilot and air leader, flying in North Africa was very different from combat over the Channel or Northern France. Therefore, he was initially attached to 145 Squadron to gain experience of Desert Air Force activities. He also met the man from whom he would take over, Wing Commander John Darwen, Officer Commanding No 244 Wing, DAF.

One pilot in 145 Squadron who remembers Gleed's arrival was Dennis Usher, then a sergeant pilot. The day before the new wing commander designate arrived, Usher had attacked a Messerschmitt 109 which was on the tail of a Spitfire. The 109 crashed into the sea off Tamet.

Wing Commander Gleed joined 145 Squadron on which I was serving early in 1943, to gain knowledge of the desert operations before taking command of 244 Wing. I had not met him before, but his reputation as a fighter pilot had reached us in the desert before he arrived. I flew with him on many occasions and remember him as a pugnacious man although small in stature. He soon learnt the desert techniques. He was well liked on the squadron which was very cosmopolitan, having (over the first months of 1943) an American CO, one Rhodesian, one New Zealand and one Polish flight commander, the rest being Australian, South African, Canadian and about three or four Englishmen.

When Gleed arrived in North Africa, the Allied armies were fast establishing themselves at the western end of the Mediterranean following the American and British 'Torch' landings on the coast of Algiers. Following more than two years of bitter fighting in Libya and the Western Desert against both the Italians and Germans, victory seemed to be finally in sight. Since November 1942 when General Bernard Montgomery had launched his tremendous offensive from his defence line at El Alamein at the eastern end of the desert, which had swept all before it, the pressure had been on. At the western end, in French North Africa (Algiers), the invasion there, also in November, caught the Axis forces between the two Allied fronts.

The British 1st and 8th Armies pushed forward quickly, eating up the miles of sand which covered the Western Desert, Libya and on towards Southern Tunisia. From Algiers the forces under General Dwight Eisenhower had moved steadily eastwards towards Tunisia. Rommel and his famous and so nearly victorious Afrika Korps, together with the Germans' Axis partners, the Italians, had gradually been squeezed into Tunisia. Harried from both sides, with air superiority almost completely lost and with precious supplies, especially fuel oils, being stopped by Malta's offensive actions, their situation was becoming desperate.

Montgomery's forces had reached Tripoli at the beginning of 1943, as the Axis troops fell back into Southern Tunisia. Their plan was to make a stand in the old French defensive positions at Mareth, built during the 1930's. Monty's air cover was the very competent Desert Air Force. Experienced, long suffering, determined, capable and competent, the DAF had come a long way since its formation with virtually obsolete biplanes at the beginning of the war. Now, in 1943, the front line DAF units comprised the following units: one fighter and two fighter-bomber wings with a third fighter-bomber wing in reserve. The fighter wing, Number 244, shouldered the task of maintaining air superiority, in which the fighter-bomber squadrons could operate. These fighter-bomber wings were, 239 Wing (250, 260, 450 and 3 RAAF Squadrons flying Curtis P40 Kittyhawks) and the American 57th Fighter Group (64th, 65th, and 66th Fighter Squadrons equipped with P40F Warhawks), to whom 112 Squadron RAF was attached also flying Kittyhawks. The third fighter-bomber wing, which was resting at this time was 7 South African Air Force Wing (2, 4 and 5 SAAF Squadrons).

No 244 Wing, which Gleed would soon lead, comprised 92, 145, 601 and 1 SAAF Squadrons, plus 73 Squadron flying Hurricane night-fighters. The four day fighter squadrons were equipped with Spitfire Vb and Spitfire Vc machines. Other DAF units were 40 SAAF Squadron for tactical reconnaissance (Tac/R) sorties, while deeper photographic missions were carried out by 2 PRU Squadron (Spitfire IVs) and 1437 Strategic Reconnaissance Flight

Tunisia 1943

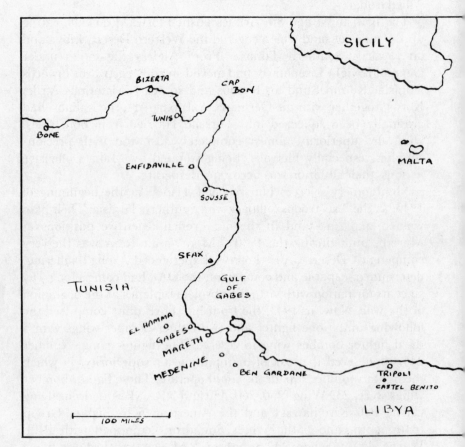

(Baltimores). 89 Squadron carried out night-fighter operations with Bristol Beaufighters. 6 Squadron RAF and 7 SAAF Squadrons had 'tank-busting Hawker Hurricane IIDs, armed with 40 mm cannons under their wings, plus 46 and 252 Squadrons with Beaufighters for long range interdiction missions.

Opposing these fighter forces of the Desert Air Force were all three Gruppen of Jagdeschwader 77 led by Major Joachim Muncheberg who had flown in France, over England, Russia and the desert. He held the Knight's Cross with Oak Leaves and Swords and had 122 combat victories. His I Gruppe was commanded by Hauptmann Heinz Bär, also a Knight's Cross holder and with over 100 victories. II Gruppe was commanded by Hauptmann Anton Hackl, like Bär a 100 victory man with the Knight's Cross, while III Gruppe was head by Hauptmann Kurt Ubben with 97 victories, the Knight's Cross with Oak Leaves.

Under their command were a number of expert Luftwaffe fighter pilots, many with over 50 victories. JG77 flew Messerschmitt 109F fighters.

There was also a ground attack unit, flying Me109s, 1/SG.2 and I and III Gruppen of SG/3 equipped with Ju87D Stuka dive bombers. The Italian Regia Aeronautica was also a fighter force to be reckoned with, flying Macchi fighters. Axis bombers were mostly Staffels of Junkers 88.

No 145 Squadron, to which Gleed was attached, was commanded by Squadron Leader Roy Marples DFC and bar. He had seen action over Dunkirk, during the Battle of Britain and in sweeps over France, flying initially with 616 Squadron, then later as a flight commander with 41 Squadron. Coming to the desert in 1942 he had flown with 127 Squadron before commanding 238 Squadron. He took over 145 shortly before receiving the bar to his DFC in December 1942.

Marples welcomed Gleed to the desert and to his squadron, imparting as much knowledge as he had himself acquired to the new wing commander. Gleed also talked to but listened equally to 145's two experienced flight commanders, John Stuart Taylor and Lance Wade DFC and bar. Taylor had been with the squadron since mid-1942 and although he had only personally destroyed three enemy aircraft and shared a fourth, he had in addition,

probably destroyed or damaged a further seven. He was awarded
the DFC at about the time of Gleed's arrival, and had, like Dennis
Usher, destroyed an enemy fighter only the day before – the 12th.
(Roy Marples too had shot down a hostile aircraft on the 12th, a
Macchi, but when his own engine cut out he had to force-land on
the sea. He was rescued by two soldiers who swam out to him.)
Lance Wade was an American from Texas, who had just returned
to the desert following a visit home. When he left the previous
autumn he had 15 victories, gained in just a year with 33 Squadron.
He was already being called 'Wildcat' Wade by his desert
companions and not without cause – he was a superb fighter pilot.

Of the other squadrons in 244 Wing, 92 Squadron was
commanded by Squadron Leader John Milne Morgan DFC who
had been in 238 Squadron with Marples, rising eventually to
command a flight. When 92 Squadron arrived in the desert from
England he took over a flight with them. In December he was given
command of the unit and received a well earned DFC. When Gleed
arrived he had seven victories. 92's flight commanders were Flight
Lieutenants W. L. Chisholm DFC and C. J. 'Sammy' Samouelle DFC.

No 601 Squadron was commanded by Squadron Leader George
H.F. Plinston, a pre-war pilot who had seen action in France in
1940 with 607 Squadron. Over Dunkirk he flew with 242 Squadron.
In 1942 he was with 3 RAAF Squadron in North Africa flying
Kittyhawks during the battle of El Alamein. Later he went to 250
Squadron before taking command of 601, having gained seven
victories. 1 SAAF Squadron was under the command of Squadron
Leader Peter Olver DFC. Pete Olver was British and had flown
during the Battle of Britain with 603 Squadron and then 66
Squadron in 1941. He was another pilot to fly in 238 Squadron in
North Africa in 1942 before being given command of 213 Squadron.
During one period when the Germans were retreating from El
Alamein, he had led 213 from a secret airstrip deep in the desert
behind the enemy lines. From this landing ground they harried the
German transport columns and during an attack on a German
airfield at Agedabia, Olver destroyed three aircraft on the ground.
He was an extremely experienced desert fighter when he was put in
command of 1 SAAF Squadron in November 1942.

Ian Gleed made his first flight with 145 Squadron the day following his arrival. At 4.30 pm on 14 January he took up Spitfire EP309 for an hour, doing some local flying to familiarise himself with the locality.

The following day the British 8th Army began its assault on the enemy's Buerat Line, but the Germans, under Field Marshal Erwin Rommel, pulled back to the Homs/Tarhuna Line rather than begin a major conflict. Probably they were helped on their way by fighter-bomber attacks by Kittyhawks escorted by six aircraft of 145 Squadron, including Gleed, again flying EP309 for his first operational sortie with the Desert Air Force. Gleed then took over EP650 which he continued to fly for the rest of January.

On the 16th Gleed and five others were scrambled at 11.05 am when Me109s were seen over the front but they failed to engage. That afternoon Gleed led ten Spitfires in a fighter sweep in support of Kittyhawks bombing Tauorga. Gleed's Spitfires flew at 17,000 feet, and when west of Sedada four Messerschmitt 109s were seen above. Gleed warned his pilots and tried to climb up to them but the German pilots were not feeling playful at those odds, and climbed away. Four of 145's pilots fired at them but they made no claims.

Another escort sortie to Kittyhawks on the morning of the 20th was followed by two further missions on the 21st. On this day the British forces broke through the German defences at Corradini, advancing to within fifty miles of Tripoli.

Twelve aircraft of 145 took off at 10.30 am on a sweep over Tripoli at 10,000 feet. Near Castel Benito the formation was attacked by five enemy fighters, identified as German Me109s and Italian Macchi 202s. They dived down from 12,000 feet but Gleed saw them and broke towards the enemy. Three immediately broke away but the other two pressed home their attacks, making a determined pass against the Spitfires. One Messerschmitt snapped out a burst of cannon fire at one section, then passed to the port of them. Gleed, not in the best position for an attack, nevertheless winged over as the 109 swooped over and by the Spits. Although at a disadvantage, Gleed opened his throttle and turned after the German, firing a longish burst after the rapidly disappearing Messerschmitt but observed no results from his fire. The other 109 too kept going and soon both 109s were out of range and diving fast into a ground haze.

On their return to base, Gleed heard that Pete Olver and his 1 SAAF, who had been escorting Kittyhawks, had attacked three Italian fighters near Castel Verde; Olver and Captain J.H. Gaynor each claimed one destroyed, while Lieutenant D.S. Rogan probably destroyed the third.

It was proving to be a busy day for the DAF squadrons. Not long after 145 returned, Wing Commander Darwen led 12 machines of 92 Squadron to continue the patrolling of Tripoli and Castel Benito. Near the latter location several Ju87s were found dive bombing Allied positions and 92 attacked. Flying Officer Neville Duke shot down one in flames, his twelfth victory, and four other pilots claimed probables. Neville Duke took command of a flight of the squadron following this mission when Samouelle was rested. Duke also received a bar to his DFC.

In the afternoon Kittyhawks bombed and strafed road transport on the Zuara-Tripoli road then, finding more than 50 enemy aircraft on the aerodrome of Castle Benito, attacked this also. The report of these aircraft led Group HQ to order a further strike against them, a protective air umbrella being provided for the fighter-bombers by nine aircraft of 145 Squadron, led by Gleed. Widge took the Spitfires in a wide sweep over Cap Bon at 8,000 feet and as he looked down he saw more than 30 German and Italian aeroplanes on the Cap Bon landing ground. On their third sweep over this landing area, Gleed spotted a German Fieseler Fi156 'Storch' light observation machine gathering speed prior to take off. Gleed did a wing over and peeled off towards it. It proved a slow and difficult target for the diving Spitfire, Gleed's first burst missing the Storch. However, the German pilot quickly lost interest and hurriedly landed again. Gleed put his Spitfire into a turn but some Kittyhawks were making a dive-bombing attack so he pulled up and away.

A short time later he saw either the same or another Fieseler airborne and for a second time Gleed lost height to attack. However, heavy return fire from the ground came up, shells exploding about him and tracer trying to seek him out, so he decided to leave the tempting but slow and obviously well protected Storch and climbed up and away from the intense AA fire. One wonders who it was who appeared so persistent in trying to take-off in the Fieseler while Spitfires patrolled nearby and Kittyhawks bombed the airfield. Continuing the patrol, Gleed and the others saw a further squadron of Kittyhawks attack the field, observing one Heinkel 111 bomber set on fire.

Gleed was in the air twice the next day, 22 January, leading a formation on a sweep over Tripoli in the morning and a six-man sweep over the same area that afternoon; Wildcat Wade flew with him on the latter sortie. Below them the Germans were leaving Tripoli for the last time, evacuating westwards.

One or two changes took place in 244 Wing at or near the end of January. On the 26th Roy Marples became tour-expired and handed over 145 Squadron to Lance Wade who was promoted to squadron leader. Shortly afterwards Squadron Leader J.M. Morgan also became due for a rest, his place being taken by Squadron Leader William John Harper, a pre-war pilot who had been a flight commander with 17 Squadron in the Battle of Britain. Also on the 26th, Flight Lieutenant Derek F. Westrana DFC took over B Flight in 601 Squadron. 'Jerry' Westrana, a New Zealander, was yet another extremely experienced desert air fighter, having also seen action in Greece in 1941 and then on Crete. He had been with 112 Squadron and by January 1943 had accounted for at least six German and Italian aircraft.

Following the capture of Tripoli and the nearby air base complex of Castel Benito, there was something of a lull on the southern, Desert Air Force, front. The main air activity was concentrated around the central area and in the north. It was also a time for several DAF squadrons to move their bases further westward to keep up with the Allied advance, now that the enemy had pulled back to Mareth.

Castel Benito, Mussolini's great pre-war prestige aerodrome, became the home of several DAF units over the next few days. The aerodrome was littered with the sad wrecks of many German and Italian aeroplanes, a sight which was fast becoming commonplace in the North African campaign. 601 Squadron moved up to Darragh North landing ground for a while before they, Gleed and 145 Squadron, moved to Castel Benito, followed by 92 Squadron a short time later, and then 1 SAAF Squadron. Gleed managed to 'liberate' a small two-door Italian Fiat car for his personal use, and also a command trailer which had previously been used by a

German Kommandant. He did, of course, have his own Ford trailer when he took over 244 Wing. It had a bed, table and chair, a small toilet, a radio and several shelves and small cupboards.

The DAF squadrons were now leaving the sandy desert landscape over which it had flown and fought for so long. Reaching into southern Tunisia the colour of the terrain changed to green and further north they flew over wooded hills and arable land.

Much to the delight of all the wing's squadron commanders, they met and were introduced to the Prime Minister, Mr Winston Churchill, at Castel Benito on 4 February during the great man's visit while on his Middle East tour. It was a strange turn of events which led Ian Gleed to meet the man who had signed his father's Mention in Despatches certificate, 25 years earlier.

On 5 February Pete Olver handed over command of 1 SAAF Squadron to a South African pilot, Major D.D. Moodie DFC, who had previously commanded No 4 SAAF Squadron and seen considerable action. Olver became 244 Wing's OC Flying taking over from Squadron Leader Young. John Darwen was still the wing leader but Ian Gleed was fast becoming proficient and it would not be long before he relieved Darwen in the leadership.

Gleed's first operational sortie from Castel Benito was flown on the afternoon of 8 February, a sweep over southern Tunisia, but generally things remained quiet on the southern front. For the next few days 145 Squadron even had time to fly some practice formations, something it had not done for many weeks. It also moved to Wadi Sirru for a short stay before returning to Castel Benito on the 16th. It was also on the 16th that the 8th Army entered Ben Gardane and Medenine just south of Mareth, which signalled the start, albeit slowly, of some renewed air activity for the DAF.

Two days later Gleed became leader of 244 Wing upon John Darwen's end of tour (although the Air Ministry dates 31 January as the day Gleed officially took command). Gleed now had his personal initials painted on the side of his Spitfire, IR-G, to add to his Figaro mascot. Perhaps the establishment of 244 Wing in Tunisia should be made clear at this stage. It consisted of a commanding officer with the rank of wing commander who had full administrative command of the wing as a self contained mobile unit. His number two, holding the rank of squadron leader, was responsible for the wing flying and operational duties. As previously mentioned, this latter post had just been filled by Squadron Leader Peter Olver DFC. To the reader the situation might become slightly confused for, as we shall see, Ian Gleed carried out a great deal of operational flying although not strictly required to do so! Later the establishment was raised so that a group captain commanded a wing while a wing commander became wing leader and OC Flying. By that time it was rare for the leader, ie the group captain, to take an active part in operations.

That same day, 18 February, Gleed took off in EP550 at 3.20 pm in company with Flight Lieutenant J.S. Taylor, plus two Spitfires from 1 SAAF and two other wing aircraft, to carry out an important escort duty. A Lockheed Hudson, carrying Air Chief Marshal Sir W. Sholto Douglas to Malta, needed air escort and 244 Wing, led by Gleed, was handed the task. This his first assignment following command of the wing, did not begin well for initially they began to escort the wrong Hudson! Quickly realising the mistake, the Spitfires landed back at 1 SAAF's base, sorted out the error, were rapidly airborne again and this time successfully escorted the right Hudson to the island fortress of Malta, landing their at 5.25 pm. They stayed the night on the famous island, Gleed leading his pilots back to Castel Benito the following morning.

He immediately threw himself into the exacting task of leading his wing, not from the ground as he could easily have done, but from the air. It would not even occur to a man like Gleed to lead it any other way. On the 21st he led 1 SAAF, in company with 92 and 145, flying on either side, in line abreast, but stepped up slightly. Detaching four Spitfires as previously arranged, these four carried out dummy attacks on the main formation. Gleed was back in the training role. One change introduced by the new wing leader was that during a wing turn, the inner and outer squadrons would both cross over above the leader, but that the inner squadron crossed above the outer squadron. This same tactic he also applied when a squadron was flying in sections. [See diagram over page.]

Weather on the southern DAF front restricted missions during this period but it improved slightly on the 22nd. Two Spitfires of 145 Squadron scrambled to intercept a reconnaissance Ju88. Flight Lieutenant Taylor and Sergeant R.T. Breheny both attacked, claiming it as damaged.

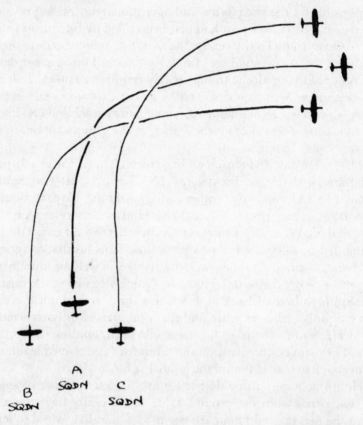

The 8th Army was now preparing for its assault on the Mareth Line which began on 26 February. Two days before Gleed flew from Castel Benito up to Medenine, just south of Mareth where 92 and 145 Squadrons had recently established their base. (1 SAAF had also moved, to Hazbub.) The Luftwaffe reacted quite strongly to the DAF's occupation of the airfield at Hazbub and for some days flew very aggressively against it. On the day the offensive opened, the 26th, Me109s strafed the base an hour before midday and as the attack ended, 145 Squadron scrambled four aircraft, headed by Gleed, the section separating once airborne. Unluckily it was not Widge and his number two which caught the Germans, but Flight Lieutenant Taylor. Taylor attacked one over Bordj Touaz, his fire tearing off the 109's starboard wing. As this went down to crash, Taylor attacked a second 109 whose pilot jettisoned his cockpit hood but as the British pilot then ran out of ammunition he was only able to claim it as a damaged.

No 145 Squadron scrambled 12 aircraft again that afternoon when bomb-carrying Me109s again attacked Hazbub airfield. Flying Officer I.H.R. Shand and his section got airborne and attacked three of them, Shand hitting one from which the pilot baled out. Flight Sergeant McKinnon damaged a second and watched it fall away and crash. Taylor claimed another as damaged but Squadron Leader Wade's Spitfire was hit by cannon shells and he was forced to make a belly landing.

It was proving the busiest day for the wing for a long time and when 601 Squadron, who had just completed its move to Hazbub Main, took off, they became involved also. At 5 o'clock they scrambled four Spitfires when more 109s were reported approaching. Ten minutes later five Messerschmitts dropped anti-personnel bombs which killed and wounded some ground crew airmen. Meanwhile, the four 601 Spitfires became embroiled in a dog-fight with the 109s, Flight Sergeant W.D. Gwynne shooting down one while Flying Officer W.M. Whitamore knocked pieces off another. Gwynne's victim was Leutnant Hugo Hauck of III/JG77 who was brought down inside Allied lines and taken prisoner.

Hazbub was again the centre of the Luftwaffe's attention the next day, Me109s attacking the airfield at 10.30 am. Eight Spitfires of 601 were already airborne to meet the threat and saw the 109s coming in but before they could engage, were immediately attacked by six more 109s. Sergeant K.J. Lusty was hit but managed to crash land at base, while Flight Lieutenant J.H. Nicholls' machine was also shot up. Gleed and four pilots of 145 were scrambled at 1.35 pm but failed to engage.

On the first day of March 1943, it was 92 Squadron's turn to see action, five of their aircraft being scrambled to engage some Macchi 202s. Neville Duke attacked the escort, shooting down two, both pilots taking to their parachutes to become prisoners. Squadron Leader Wade led 145 Squadron as escort to Kittyhawks attacking targets north of the Mareth Line that afternoon. German fighters intervened, Flight Lieutenant Taylor shooting down one Me109, Wade claiming another. Warrant Officer E.A. Ker was also credited with the destruction of a third Messerschmitt.

Hazbub Main did not remain free of attention for long; it

became increasingly apparent that the Germans wanted the squadrons using it to depart. As 109 fighter-bomber attacks had so far failed, another tactic was employed. At 4.50 pm German artillery shells began to rain down on the landing ground from nearby hills. Gleed, without a moment's hesitation, ordered 601 Squadron to get their Spitfires away to El Assa and Zuara, the pilots making their take-off runs amid heavy shelling. The enemy fire was accurate and incessant, one shell exploding under Flight Sergeant Reynolds' machine as he took off, forcing him to crash a mile or so away, badly injured. The squadron later reformed at Ben Gardane.

Forty minutes after Hazbub was hit by the first shells, Medenine was on the receiving end of Axis shelling. 92 and 145 Squadrons being forced to make a hurried evacuation back to Castel Benito. Two Spitfires were damaged, one having to make a crash landing at Zaura. One 145 pilot took-off carrying another pilot in the cockpit. The following day the two squadrons joined 601 at Ben Gardane.

Ninety-two and 145 Squadrons flew a morning sweep on 3 March although a Spitfire of each unit collided on take-off. Not far from Gabes, 145 found several Italian Macchi 202s and damaged one. On the return flight Flight Lieutenant Duke spotted a lone Me109 near the Mareth Line and succeeded in shooting it down. Gleed was twice airborne that day, leading a sweep in the afternoon with 92 and 145 Squadrons. Later he scrambled with six aircraft of 145 but failed to contact reported raiders. These two sorties were the first in which it is known for certain he flew in Spitfire Vb, serial number AB502. An ex-145 Squadron aircraft which had been coded ZX-B, he had his ground crew paint on his initials and the Figaro motif, plus wing commander's pennant. In this Spitfire he was to fly the majority of his final operations over Tunisia – and also his last mission.

No 92 Squadron were again in action late the following afternoon during a patrol above the Mareth Line and again it was Neville Duke who found the enemy. Some Me109 fighters were attacking Hazbub landing ground but Duke's interference cost the Luftwaffe two machines; one pilot was seen to bale out.

Gleed and his new Figaro flew one mission on the 4th, leading 145 Squadron on an escort to bomb-carrying Kittyhawks. 92 and 1

27.   Widge with his 'liberated' Italian Fiat car at Castel Benito aerodrome. Abandoned Italian aeroplanes littered the airfield.

28.   A welcome mug of tea for Gleed and Pete Olver at Castel Benito. The two hatted men are army officers.

29. *(Above)* Wing Commander Ian Gleed in Figaro (AB502) taken shortly before his death. This official Air Ministry Publicity photograph was released for publication on April 15, 1943 the day before Gleed flew his last mission.

30. Ian Gleed's final resting place at Enfidaville Military cemetary, Tunisia. This original cross was replaced in 1958 by the more familiar military style concrete headstone.

SAAF plus 601, were all busy during the 5th, 92 flying top cover to the South Africans. 92, however, were attacked by seven Messerschmitts of I/JG77, Hauptmann Heinz Bär shooting down Sergeant 'Happy' McMahon. Eight machines of 601 flew up to Hazbub Main for forward readiness and scrambled four of them just after mid-day to patrol over the forward area. A lone 109 was engaged, the pilot being the same Heinz Bär who had shot down McMahon that morning. Bär attacked 601, forcing Flight Sergeant Tilston to bale out. During a later scramble by 601, one Spitfire was caught in another's slipstream and hit the ground, injuring the pilot.

Early the following day 145 Squadron escorted Kittyhawks attacking Axis columns north of Medenine, two 109s being damaged in a brief dog-fight. Two hours later, at 8.50 am, Gleed led eight aircraft of 601 for a reconnaissance mission. Taking off from Ben Gardane South Landing Ground (in EP966 not AB502) they flew at zero feet to reconnoitre the landing grounds at Gabes and El Hamma. They flew north-east, crossed the coast so as to approach Gabes from across the Gulf of the same name, before proceeding further inland to El Hamma. Flight Sergeant J.E. Robinson, a Canadian, flying ER317, off to one side hit the sea, his Spitfire breaking up and sinking. He undoubtedly misjudged his height while flying so low and no sign of him was found.

Squadron Leader Wade led his squadron into a fight with some 109s and Mc202s later that day, the Texan forcing one to belly-land, then shot pieces off another. Sergeant Usher damaged two Ju87s he found on the edge of the battle while Pilot Officer M.L. Lawrence-Smith sent an enemy fighter into the sea. The wing was also in action a short time later when aircraft of 601 and 1 SAAF, on patrol, ran into 28 Ju87s plus escorting 109s. Major Moodie and Lieutenant Tyrell destroyed one; Tyrell probably destroyed another. To end another busy day, 145 encountered several twin-engined Me210s and damaged one as the sun went down, while Flight Sergeant A.A. Toller of 601 who had been engaged on a further recce of Gabes and El Hamma LGs, was repeatedly attacked by a very persistent Kittyhawk until he eventually had to crash-land.

If 6 March had been busy for the DAF and for 244 Wing, Sunday the 7th was even busier. 145 were off at 9.20 am to fly a patrol over the battle front, finding six Italian fighters north of Medenine. Sergeant Usher shot one down, another pilot claiming another as a probable. Gleed led 1 SAAF on another patrol but again saw nothing.

At 11 o'clock the wing leader led six Spitfires of 145 out on a patrol to be followed at 11.35 am by six of 1 SAAF. Just before mid-day, Gleed spotted a dozen Messerschmitt 109s and Macchi 202s and he expertly brought his formation round to make a surprise attack. Gleed swooped down on the enemy formation who began to break just as the diving Spitfires came within range. Gleed turned after one Messerschmitt, then from astern and at 200 yards range, opened fire with both cannon and machine-guns. His shells and bullets splattered over the 109, striking cannon shells blasting pieces off the German fighter which immediately nosed over and disappeared into some clouds four miles east of Maret.

Glancing quickly over his shoulder he saw four 109s coming down after him and he rapidly banked Figaro towards them and called for assistance over the R/T. His call was answered by 1 SAAF who had already spotted the dog-fight between 145 and the Messerschmitts, and had begun to join in. Lieutenant Fouche heard the wing leader's call, attacked the four pursuing fighters, damaged one and drove off the others. Flight Lieutenant Taylor (in EP199) shot down a Macchi 202 which crashed into the sea and Sergeant J.E. Parker (EP193), like Gleed, succeeded in damaging a 109. The South Africans also damaged some of their opponents and on the way home shot up a Ju88, one of 12 they found bombing Neffatia airfield.

Not to be left out of the action, 92 Squadron on patrol over Medenine, found three Me109s below them. Duke shot down one while Flight Lieutenant Hunk Humphreys and Sergeant M.W.H. Askey claimed another between them. Later that afternoon 92 were scrambled and intercepted 20 Me109s near Neffatia, Duke seeing his opponent bale out. 145 also got themselves airborne, John Taylor leading the attack on ten 109s and like Duke he hit one so badly its pilot took to his parachute.

Gleed flew another patrol with Peter Olver and four pilots of 1 SAAF, and saw a lone Me109G stalking some Kittyhawks. Gleed led his men towards the German but the enemy pilot saw them and throttling forward, rapidly outdistanced the Spitfire Vs with his superior 109G. Gleed was in the air again the next morning leading a patrol of 145 Squadron over the forward area.

Focke Wulf 190s were seen for the first time over North Africa on the 8th and engaged by Hunk Humphreys and Pilot Officer G. Wilson of 92 Squadron, although they made no claims. Squadron Leader Wade damaged a 109 following a scramble from Hazbub, and Dennis Usher received a commission to pilot officer.

No 601 Squadron shot down a reconnaissance 109 on 10 March during a chance encounter whilst escorting 'tank-busting' Hurricanes of 6 Squadron. Gleed flew with 601 as top cover to Kittyhawks on the afternoon of the 10th, 601 being led by Jerry Westrana. Also on this date, 145 and 1 SAAF moved to Bu Grara airfield, to be followed by 601 on the 11th. On the 12th Squadron Leader George Plinston of 601 Squadron, received the DFC.

The following day 92 Squadron provided top cover to American P40s of the 57th Fighter Group. JG77 intercepted them and although 92 engaged the attacking Messerschmitts, destroying one and damaging two more, the Americans lost four P40s. In their fight the P40s claimed three 109s. Flight Lieutenant Chisholm DFC and bar, of 92 Squadron, ended his tour; his place was taken by Flight Lieutenant E.A.G.C. Bruce.

On Sunday the 14th Gleed led seven aircraft from 145 as top cover to Kittyhawks during a mid-day fighter bomber attack on enemy positions and the next afternoon he, John Taylor and another pilot flew cover escort to a further Kittyhawk attack. Wednesday, 17 March again proved a busy day for the DAF squadrons; 601 became embroiled in an air battle it saw in progress above Medenine. They succeeded in damaging a couple of 109s, and when some Stukas appeared Warrant Officer D.G. Gordon sent one down pouring out black smoke. Lieutenant B.R. Bennetts was not so fortunate, failing to return. It was later confirmed that he was both wounded and a prisoner.

Twelve Spitfires of 92 scrambled shortly after mid-day to intercept bomb-carrying 109s escorted by other Messerschmitts and Macchi 202s. Two of the enemy fighters were hit but Pilot Officer Paul Brickhill was attacked and shot down by a Macchi. The Italian pilot's fire hit his mainplane, exploding the ammunition bay. This future successful author was forced to take to his parachute and was taken prisoner. In fact his victor may have been a 109 pilot although the squadron's records indicate it was a Macchi 202.

On the afternoon of the 17th a Desert Air Force Commander's Conference was arranged at 57 Group's Headquarters. The object was to brief all unit commanders on the coming final offensive against the Mareth Line. Gleed and Figaro took off for the ten minute flight to the HQ at 2.30 pm in company with his OC Flying, Pete Olver and the CO of 145, Lance Wade. After the conference, they took off to return at 4.45 pm but Gleed and Olver decided to have a practice dog-fight; the two Spitfire pilots gambolled happily in the afternoon sunshine. Then over the radio came the voice of the controller at Command HQ, informing them that 'snappers' (enemy fighters) were in their vicinity. Searching the sky, Olver acting as Gleed's number two, the two fighter pilots quickly spotted two Messerschmitt 109Gs. They had also seen the two Spitfires and with their superior performance machines, immediately changed course towards them, coming in head-on. Gleed and Olver easily evaded their pass and, as Gleed later stated: 'This led to a pleasant, hard-running dog-fight back to the German lines.'

Luckily on this occasion, the two experienced British air fighters managed to stay with the 109s, and Widge got the rear Messerschmitt squarely in his gun sight and fired. He continued:

'I managed to shoot down one Messerschmitt at a range of 100 yards. It crashed in enemy territory.'

The 109G actually crashed on a beach just north of the enemy's front line. Gleed and Olver returned to base, landing at 5.05 pm – just twenty minutes after taking off from the conference.

Following the evening meal Gleed visited 1 SAAF Squadron's mess to inform them of the impending offensive. He gave the South Africans a pep talk on tactics and stressed to the pilots the importance of keeping complete air superiority to cover the advancing Allied troops.

One other item of interest occurred on the 17th, this being the arrival of the Polish Fighting Team which was attached to 145 Squadron. They became operational as an independent unit under the command of Squadron Leader S.F. Skalski DFC and bar. Stanislaw Skalski, a veteran Polish fighter pilot, had fought the Germans in the skies of Poland, during the Battle of Britain and during operations over Northern France in 1941-42. With him he had brought fifteen volunteers, taken from various Polish squadrons and the team was soon being called 'Skalski's Circus'. Gleed welcomed the addition of the Polish pilots to his wing. He had had several Poles attached to 87 Squadron for short periods in 1941 and admired their aggressive fighting spirit.

Bad weather prevented the full scale attack upon the Mareth Line after the conference, but ground activity resumed on the 20th. 1 SAAF was scrambled during the morning finding Messerschmitts, Macchis and the new FW190s. The enemy fighters were completely disorganised by the South Africans as they dived upon them, and although they scattered and tried to retreat, Lieutenant J.R. Lanham shot down one Focke Wulf, the first to be shot down over this part of the front. Gleed and Olver, plus five pilots of 92 Squadron plus two sections of 145, escorted Kittyhawks during an attack on El Hamma at 11.30 am.

Squadron Leader George Plinston, CO of 601 Squadron, ended his tour on the 20th; his place was taken by John Taylor of 145 Squadron. Taylor's place as B Flight commander in 145 was taken by Flying Officer I.H. Shand.

Gleed was scrambled twice on the 21st, once at 4.30 pm in company with aircraft of 92 Squadron, but they saw nothing. He landed back at 5.25 pm, but ten minutes later he was off again with 1 SAAF and ordered up to 15,000 feet above Mareth. However, the enemy aircraft turned back. The Spitfires received the usual 'hate' from ground gunners, and Major Moodie's Spitfire was hit and damaged.

Heavy rain restricted air activity the next day but it failed to dampen Ian Gleed's determination to be in the air whenever possible. On three separate occasions he scrambled alone to go after reported enemy aircraft, at 10.05, 1 o'clock and 4.15 pm. He also flew a mission with 92 Squadron during the day. Sadly his efforts did not produce any results as he failed to find enemy aircraft on each occasion.

John Taylor, leading 601 for the first time during the day over Gabes, shot down one Me109, and Pilot Officer D. Ibbotson another, both being credited as probables. Wade and 145 were scrambled twice, meeting JG77, Wade destroying one of the 109s,

Pilot Officer Hanley a second.

The next day, the 23rd, Gleed sent twelve of his pilots to Algiers in a Hudson to collect new Spitfire Mark IXs. Flying back with the first IXs to reach the Desert Air Force, six going to Skalski's Poles and four to 92 Squadron. Gleed was again in action on the 24th, scrambling alone with Figaro twice at 10.15 and 3.15 pm, then again at 4.50 in company with Flight Sergeant Anderson and Sergeant E.A. Stott of 145, but again no contact was made. Flight Lieutenant Shand, however, managed to destroy a 109 during the day.

New Zealand troops supported by the 8th Armoured Brigade attacked enemy positions at 4 pm on the 26th. In the air they were supported by Kittyhawks and above them flew Gleed's Spitfires. After this mission, Gleed was off again (in EN186 a Spitfire IX for the first time – Figaro being grounded for a service), in company with Flight Lieutenant Waclaw Krol and two other pilots of Skalski's Circus. They covered the opening of the attack on the Tebaga Gap.

All the wing aircraft were busy over the next few days, escorting Kittyhawks or fighting off enemy fighters over the front. Losses occurred on both sides but the ground attack progressed. Gleed led a sweep over Sfax at 10.15 on the 28th again in a Spitfire IX, in company with six machines of 145 flying top cover to 601. They reconnoitered El Maou but then near Sfax at 8,000 feet they saw seven Ju88s flying at zero feet. Gleed, knowing how anxious the Poles were to get in amongst them, ordered two Spitfires of the Team down, flown by Skalski (in EN459) and Flight Lieutenant Eugeniusz Horbaczewski (EN267). Skalski attacked one which he hit in the wing whereupon it rolled over and crashed into some buildings. Horbaczewski got behind a second 88 which crashed with both of its engines blazing. It was the Polish Team's first victories and proved the value of the superior performance of the Spitfire Mark IX. Meanwhile, 601 saw some other Ju88s taking off from Gafsa and attacked. They shot down one plus a lone Me109 flying as escort. Later in the day, Gleed flew on an escort mission to Kittyhawks with 145 Squadron, and ended the day with an air test on Figaro.

March came to an end for Gleed with three further sorties, a lone patrol over Sfax and Gabes between 6.05 and 8.15 am on the 29th, a sweep with four aircraft of 145 over Sfax and Zitouna mid-morning of the 30th, and a lone scramble on the afternoon of the 31st. One pleasant event for Ian Gleed was a letter he received on the 29th, personally notifying him of the award of the Belgian Croix de Guerre.

The Spitfire IXs made another kill on the 29th when Pilot Officers F.R. Barker and M.L. Lawrence-Smith of 145 Squadron shot down a Ju88 south of Zitouna. Meanwhile, a lower flight of 145 flying Vbs engaged enemy fighters, Wildcat Wade destroying two 109s to bring his personal score to 19 which won for him a second bar to his DFC. At 11.25 am 92 Squadron were engaged by six Me109Gs but they reversed the situation, Duke and Flying Officer T. 'Doc' Savage each destroying one. It was Duke's twentieth victory.

On the ground the enemy had been pushed back to Wadi Akarit but the New Zealanders were attacking the outposts of this line by the 30th. With March at an end the new month was bound to see further assaults against the German's rapidly diminishing territory in Tunisia. The enemy was now hard pressed although its fighting men, especially its air force, were still resisting most vigorously. However, the Allies were confident that success was near. Indeed success and victory was near although the leader of 244 Wing, whose cheerful spirit often encouraged his pilots, was not destined to see it. Wing Commander Ian Gleed had just sixteen days of life left to him.

CHAPTER THIRTEEN

A Leader to the end

I remember him as a delightful personality exuding cheerfulness even in trying times, a fearless fighter pilot and an individual who stood out even amongst the many stalwart characters in that fighter force.

So recalls Air Chief Marshal Sir Frederick Rosier GCB CBE DSO, who was, in early 1943, Wing Commander Operations and second-in-command of 211 Group in North Africa. This is exactly how many DAF men remember Ian Gleed, the diminutive 'air hog' who seemed to be always in the air leading his wing or exuding confidence to his men at briefings or at times of relaxation while on the ground. Another air leader who remembers him is Air Chief Marshal Sir Harry Broadhurst GCB KBE DSO DFC AFC, who was in command of the Desert Air Force in 1943.

Widge Gleed was killed shortly after he came out to the desert to command 244 Wing. He was at that time leading his wing as top cover for a rather elaborate operation we had set up to intercept German reinforcements of fuel and ammunition – and I believe some troops – in Ju52s just before the end of the Tunisian Campaign. I remember the occasion vividly, because it was highly successful and I believe Widge Gleed was one of the few losses we had and it saddened the occasion. He was a splendid little chap whom I was delighted to get and very sad to lose after such a short time under my command.

Ian Gleed had now been in the Royal Air Force for seven years and was a most experienced pilot. Except for a few months at the end of 1942 he had been almost constantly on operations since May

1940. He was about to begin his thirtieth month of operational flying.

As wing commander of 244 Wing he was, as already explained, not really expected to fly as much as he did, but Gleed being Gleed this did not mean anything to him. For a man who did not need to fly so much, April 1943, or to be precise, in the first sixteen days of it, he flew at least once every day except two and on one of those days nobody flew. During those last sixteen days he flew at least fourteen missions – probably more.

Neville Duke, the wing's top scoring fighter pilot as at the beginning of April 1943, remembers Ian Gleed at that time:

> Ian Gleed was a highly respected and admired wing leader during his time with 244 Wing. He was a most aggressive fighter pilot who inspired the utmost devotion with his leadership. He had a somewhat boyish enthusiasm, but with authority – an ideal leader in the Desert Air Force where respect for one's leaders was judged by their operational ability. Withall he was an officer and gentleman in the true sense. He was a great loss.

Gleed's busy last month began at 8.30 am on the morning of Thursday, 1 April 1943, the RAF's 25th Anniversary. Flying with Dennis Usher and Pilot Officer M.L. Lawrence-Smith, he flew top cover to Douglas Bostons bombing enemy positions.

No 1 SAAF Squadron fought six Me109s on 2 April, destroying one; later in the day four Spitfire IXs flown by Skalski and his men fought a dozen 109s north of Gabes while escorting American P40s and bombers. Skalski shot down one into the sea while Horbaczewski destroyed another. Flight Sergeant M. Machowiak claimed a third. In the afternoon 145 escorted other American P40s damaged two Me109s who tried to intercept, and two pilots of 1 SAAF were bounced by eight 109s over Gabes but managed to outfight them and get away without injury. Gleed's only flight on the 2nd was a local trip to El Hamma.

Little activity was recorded by the wing on the following day but on the 4th Gleed led 1 SAAF on an escort to two Kittyhawk squadrons during an attack on the enemy landing ground at Zittouna and later he and Figaro were scrambled but failed to locate a reported enemy aircraft.

Skalski and his Poles managed to intercept a formation of Ju88s escorted by 109s north of Gabes, Skalski destroying one of the latter, Flight Lieutenant Waclaw Krol getting another. During the afternoon 145 provided top cover for 1 SAAF on a sweep over Mezzouna. They found several Messerschmitts. Wade destroyed one while Pilot Officer Hardy knocked another from off the Texan's tail. Lawrence-Smith made it three although his Spitfire was hit and damaged. Gleed flew a lone scramble on the 5th but again failed to find, to him, the elusive enemy.

He was again busy on the 6th flying a Spitfire IX, EN261. At 8.40 am he led 145 as top cover to 601 on a fighter sweep over the front; Gleed had Krol and four others in his section. Below them the 8th Army had opened its offensive on the Wadi Akarit Line and Gleed's wing had to keep the air clear of enemy aircraft. At 1.45 pm he led 145 again as top cover to 1 SAAF in another offensive patrol above the battle front. Then at 4.30 Gleed flew in Figaro with 92 Squadron, this time as escort to 145 Squadron. They swept the Djebel Tebaga area and when south of Cekmira three Messerschmitt 109Fs were seen. Widge flew off in pursuit but the 109s had seen the Spitfires and were pulling away. Gleed, slightly ahead of his pilots, lined up the rear 109 at extreme range. His guns rattled and his bullets blasted pieces from the Messerschmitt's tail and a thin trail of grey smoke streamed back but then the other two 109s turned to protect their comrade, flying back to attack the Allied fighters. Gleed had to pull up and bank away but Flight Lieutenant Horbaczewski shot at one and the German pilot baled out although his parachute failed to open. The other 109, however, got in a burst at the Pole and his engine caught fire. Horbaczewski half rolled prior to leaving his damaged fighter, when the fire suddenly went out, enabling him to glide safely back to Gabes.

At 10.45 am, the next morning, Gleed scrambled with 92 Squadron but they found nothing; then later at 5.35 he led a four-man patrol of 145 over Cekmira. The wing had another busy day, 145 and 601 plus Skalski's Team, all seeing action and gaining victories, but unhappily it always seemed that Gleed, whilst almost constantly in the air, was never around when the big air fights developed. He was rarely in the right place at the right time. It must have been most frustrating for a fighter of his experience and calibre to be so near and yet just miss the major actions. It may well have been this bad luck which forced him on, hoping that perhaps next time he would be at the right place. Until that happened all he could do was to help, plan, advise, encourage and lead by his force of character.

On the 8th he led a three-man patrol of 145 Squadron over the Mahares area at 10.30 am and at 5.10 pm flew in company with Pilot Officer F.R. Baker and Flight Sergeant B.E. Anderson to cover 92 Squadron on another patrol in the same area. Also during the day 1 SAAF escorted Kittyhawks bombing targets in the La Fauconnerie area, accompanied by eight Spitfire IXs of 145 and four of 92, plus Gleed and Olver's machines. 1 SAAF lost one pilot.

Two local non-operational flights visiting his squadrons occupied Widge on the 9th and 10th, while on the ground the advancing 8th Army took Sfax on the latter date. The German and Italian forces now trapped completely were becoming increasingly defensive in their decreasing territory and were desperate for fuel and other supplies from Italy. Ships could no longer get through in any number and the Axis had to resort to flying in the much needed life blood of war by transport aircraft from Italy and Sicily. Naturally these slow lumbering transports, such as Junkers 52s, Savoia-Marchetti 82s or the huge six-engined Messerschmitt 323s, were highly vulnerable to attacks by the dominant Allied fighter aircraft from both the southern and northern fronts.

On the 10th, north of Cap Bon, ten Ju52s were shot down by American twin-engined, twin-boomed P38 Lightnings, followed by the loss of at least eight more by P38s on a later mission. The massacre was continued on the 11th, when a whole formation of 20 Junkers was claimed as destroyed by American fighters.

Gleed did not fly on the 12th as far as is known (although the wing moved to La Fouconnerie and he might well have flown to the new base that day) but he was back in Figaro for a patrol over the battle area with 601 on the 13th, and what a patrol that was. His flight consisted of himself as leader, and Squadron Leader J.S. Taylor DFC, Flight Lieutenants D.F. Westrana DFC, J.H. Nicholls DFC, P.D. Thompson DFC and Flying Officer D. Ibbotson DFC. Between them they had destroyed approximately 50 enemy aircraft and it would have been extremely interesting if they had met an enemy air formation, but this was not to be. This highly experienced patrol did not meet any opposition over the front.

At 10.30 am the next morning Gleed led a wing show comprising of 1 SAAF, five of 145 as top cover and including 92 and 417 Squadrons. 417 had only now joined 244 Wing. The formation saw no enemy air activity and returned at 11.55. 417 Canadian Squadron had moved up to Goubrine South Landing Ground on the 14th and this was their first operation with the wing. It was commanded by Squadron Leader F.B. Foster who had had to be content to lead his eager Canadians on escort or patrol missions mounted from the rear until this time.

The following day Gleed visited a new landing ground before flying up to Fouconnerie to brief pilots on the following day's sorties.

No 244 Wing DAF's main opponents in Tunisia had been the Messerschmitt 109s flown by the fighter pilots of JG77. Of the pilots who fought with this unit during the first quarter of 1943, three were to be involved in the air battle in which Ian Gleed was to lose his life.

Leutnant Ernst-Wilhelm Reinert was twenty-four years old and came from Cologne. He had fought with 4/JG77 in Russia, gaining his first combat victory on 8 August 1941. By 1 July 1942 when he was awarded the Knight's Cross he had raised his number of victories to 53 and went on to add a further 29 kills to his tally before he received the Oak Leaves to his Knight's Cross. Since arriving in North Africa he had steadily increased his score, claiming Spitfires, Kittyhawks, P38 Lightnings of both RAF and USAAF units (including aircraft of 244 Wing) as well as an American B24 Liberator, a B26 Marauder and two A20s. On 13 March he had gained six victories and five on 1 April. By 16 April 1943 he had a total of 148 combat victories and only a handful of German fighter pilots had achieved more kills than him.

Flying as Reinert's wingman on 16 April was 23-year-old Heinz-Edgar Berres from Koblenz, who had been flying with JG77 since the previous year and was its I Gruppe adjutant. He had more than 40 victories, having gained at least 15 of these in Tunisia since January 1943.

Heinz Bär, at thirty years of age was the oldest of this trio. From Leipzig, 'Pritzl' Bär had been a pre-war Luftwaffe pilot and gained his first combat victory in September 1939. Flying on the Western

Front he had achieved 27 victories by July 1941 when he received his Knight's Cross. Less than two months later, flying during the early campaign on the Russian Front he brought his total to 60 to receive the Oak Leaves. He was shot down behind the Russian lines on 31 August 1941 but successfully evaded capture and made his way back to friendly territory. When he received the Swords to his Knight's Cross he had 90 victories. By April 1943 and as leader of JG77, his score was nearing 150.

On the morning of Friday, April 16, Wing Commander Ian Gleed went to the pilot's dispersal area at Goubrine South Landing Ground. Here he addressed the Canadian pilots of the recent addition to his wing, 417 Squadron. It was more than evident that the battle for Tunisia and therefore the battle of North Africa would soon be successfully concluded.

Although the Axis forces were still resisting vigorously, time, supplies and numerically superior forces must soon overwhelm them and win for the Allies a great victory. The opposing Axis forces' only hope of hanging on was the air transportation of fuel and supplies. As already related these were extremely vulnerable but the attempt had to be made. Knowing this the Allied air forces were naturally planning to intercept them as they had been doing over recent days.

As many of these transport aeroplanes flew across from Sicily low on the water, it had been agreed that the best way of intercepting them would be to fly standing patrols over the area off Cap Bon. Equally the German fighters too had begun to provide standing patrols over the sea and coastal areas of Cap Bon to intercept Allied fighters and protect their transports. Thus was the scene being irrevocably set for Ian Gleed's last air battle on the last afternoon of his life.

On the afternoon of the 16th, Gleed received instructions to provide a patrol over this area which he decided to lead himself. He selected 145 Squadron to provide the patrol with a section from 92 Squadron acting as top cover. Take-off from Goubrine South was planned for 2 o'clock (actual take-off time being recorded as 2.05 pm).

No 145 Squadron provided four Spitfire IXs and six Spitfire Vs (including Gleed's Figaro). It is of interest to note that Gleed only flew a Mark IX on a few operations. Although a superior machine over the Mark V it appears that he let others fly them, preferring the Mark V. Probably, as wing leader, he felt it better to be compelled by the slower performance to remain with the main wing formation where he was more valuable. The formation that day as listed in the squadron's records was as follows:

Spitfire V	AB502	Wing Commander I.R. Gleed DSO DFC
	ER858	Flight Sergeant J.K. Rostant
	ES315	Flying Officer P.B. Laing-Meason
	ER916	Sergeant E.A. Daley
	ES130	Flight Sergeant B.E. Anderson
	ER306	Sergeant K.D. Romain
Spitfire IX	EN239	Flight Lieutenant I.H. Shand
	EN265	Pilot Officer G.W. Small
	EN269	Pilot Officer J.I. Anderson
	EN296	Warrant Officer H. McKinnon

Flying as number two to Gleed was Flight Sergeant Rostant, a veteran Desert Air Force pilot who had been with 145 Squadron ever since Gleed had been in North Africa. He had flown with Gleed before. The three pilots of 92 Squadron, flying Spitfire IXs were:

Flight Lieutenant N.F. Duke DSO DFC
Flying Officer T. Savage
Pilot Officer G. Wilson

Neville Duke leading Black Section of 92 Squadron noted in his Log Book later that day his mission as being a 'Suicide Four' cover to 145 Squadron. This reference indicated that he was leading a flight of Spitfire IXs which were usually used to fly top cover missions to the slower Mark Vs. They would operate high above the main formation in the hope of intercepting (or bouncing) any enemy aircraft attacking the lower formation. They would also be able to warn the lower group if enemy aircraft were above them. However, this top section was itself vulnerable to attack from above and of course had no support – hence the slightly dramatic title of this type of mission.

On this occasion, Duke, flying EN333, and his two companions were flying at 20,000 feet, while Gleed and 145 were below at around 10,000 feet. Crossing the Tunisian coast they headed out over the blue waters of the Mediterranean. Shortly afterwards the experienced eyes of Neville Duke saw movement below. As he looked down he saw the shadows of a large number of aeroplanes on the sea, although at first he could not actually see the aircraft which were making them. He gazed down intently, then he saw them – enemy transport aircraft heading towards Cap Bon. He immediately called up Gleed on the radio informing the wing leader of the transports.

'Can't see them from down here,' replied Gleed, 'you lead on and we'll follow you.' Duke acknowledged and dived, followed by Savage and Wilson.

The enemy transports were now identified as 18 Ju52s and Italian SM82s (actually only SM82s were present during the action) and Duke selected one Savoia but his diving speed was too great, forcing him to overshoot. Throttling back he attacked a second Savoia flying close to the water, closed with it, fired, then roared over it just as the enemy machine hit the sea, broke up and disappeared in a huge fountain of spray. As he turned he glimpsed the Savoia's engine cowlings bouncing across the wavetops. Duke went after another 82, his fire taking immediate effect whereupon the Italian machine landed on the sea and began to sink.

With his top cover gone, Gleed and 145 were open to attack from above and far above were indeed the enemy fighters who had come out to escort the transports. However, the mass of three-engined transport aircraft took the British pilot's attention but soon the Me109s of JG77 and some FW190s were coming down to protect the lumbering transports. Duke spotted several Focke Wulfs behind him as he began to look for his third victim. Suddenly the air was full of enemy fighters.

Meanwhile his wingmen had also got amongst the transports, Doc Savage claiming two in flames while Wilson added another to make it five for 92 Squadron. As 145 Squadron came down, the Spitfire Vs went for the transports while the IXs went for the Messerschmitts.

Flight Lieutenant Shand got behind one Me109 which went into a climbing turn, Shand firing at it from 200 yards' range. The 109 went into a dive and hit the sea. Pilot Officer Small attacked two

Messerschmitts from behind, closing to 50 yards behind one of them which broke away. Small fired a long burst at the other one which staggered, went down and crashed. A FW190 attacked Small and followed him as the British pilot returned across the sea. Seeing the danger he immediately turned to make a head-on attack on the Focke Wulf but saw no results of his fire, so as his fuel was running low he broke away and once again headed for the coast. The 190 stayed with him, making a second pass, forcing Small to turn again to defend himself. This time he managed to turn inside the enemy fighter and got in two deflection bursts, his fire hitting the 190 which broke away pouring out smoke. Small turned away again and made for home, last seeing the 190 at 4,000 feet in a steep dive and smoking badly.

Warrant Officer McKinnon saw two Me109s turn above him during his approach to the transports and immediately climbed after them, attacking one from astern, closing to 100 yards, his guns rattling. The 109 rolled over, fell away and crashed. Flying Officer Laing-Meason dived into the transport aircraft, making two passes on one (which he identified as a Ju52) and saw it crash into the sea. Flight Sergeant Anderson also got amongst the transports closing to 50 yards behind one Savoia raking it with a long burst and saw it land flat on the water.

As Flight Lieutenant Duke fought for his life against a persistent FW190 he twisted and turned, grateful that he was flying a Mark IX and not a V against the Focke Wulf. Finally he put his aircraft into a steep climb and soon found himself alone. As he climbed above the battle he saw several Spitfires leaving the area and counted at least five or six SM82s down in the sea.

In those few brief moments of battle over the sea off Cap Bon, Ian Gleed was hit. What exactly happened is not fully understood but without doubt he was, like Duke, suddenly surrounded by enemy fighters. There is one report of Gleed calling for assistance but this in fact might have been Duke who remembers asking for help when the 190s struck. Duke himself remembers seeing a Spitfire shot down in flames early in the engagement and observed the pilot bale out. This had to be Flight Sergeant Rostant.

Only two Spitfires were lost, Gleed's and Rostant's. Sergeant E.A. Daley's machine was also hit and damaged but this was caused by return fire from an SM82. From the German side two

claims were made, one by Leutnant Reinert timed at 3.44 pm and
another by Leutnant Berres at 3.48 pm. (German time was an hour
ahead of British time.) Exactly who shot down which Spitfire is not
certain. Reinert claimed to have shot down a Mustang and it seems
highly possible that this was in fact Gleed's clipped-wing Spitfire
Figaro. Taking into account the times of the German pilots' claims
it looks as if Reinert selected the leading Spitfire, leaving Berres to
take the Spitfire flown by Rostant. Probably Rostant spotted the
109s, turned away from Reinert, although not quick enough to
defend his leader or defend himself from Berres. Heinz Bär also
claimed a Spitfire although neither the time or location are certain
and in any event his victim he claimed crashed into the sea. It can
be assumed that this was not Rostant as Bär made no mention of
the pilot baling out, nor could it have been Gleed, for although the
battle was fought over the sea, Widge Gleed did not go into the
water.

To add further complications to these claims, four Italian Macchi
202s were engaged in the fight while escorting the transports
(although no mention is made of any Italian fighters seen by the
surviving Allied pilots). They apparently made claims for three
Spitfires, the pilot of one being picked up by the Italian torpedo-boat
Libbra who also picked up several survivors from the shot down
SM82s.

We shall probably never know for certain what happened to Ian
Gleed during the last minutes of his life. Whether himself hit by
Reinert's or Berres' fire, it is highly probable that he was either
wounded or Figaro badly shot up and damaged, or both, for he
managed to leave the battle area and make for the Tunisian coast.
If Figaro had been hit Gleed undoubtedly tried to make for home,
probably streaming glycol, heading initially for the coast. Neville
Duke's personal diary reads:

A Flight Sergeant of 145 Squadron was shot down and baled out
OK. Sad to say Wing Commander Gleed has not returned –
probably had my experience with a lot of Huns around – last
heard calling for help.

Recalling the action and his diary note Neville Duke relates:

I have often tried to recall why it was stated at the time that the pilot who baled out was Flight Sergeant Rostant and not Ian Gleed – it seems we were not aware of his loss until he failed to return to base. I have also wondered if, in fact, the reported call for help did come from him – I did call up the rest of the formation when I was under attack, asking for assistance. I could see them withdrawing from the area but received no reply – I do not remember hearing any similar call on the R/T.

Ian Gleed and Figaro came to earth on the Tunisian coast and he either died as he came down or after he crashed – or crash landed! Life ended for him at approximately 2.50 pm on the afternoon of the 16th, just two months short of his twenty-seventh birthday.

The Spitfires of 92 and 145 Squadron returned to Goubrine to find that both Gleed and Rostant were missing. Duke reported seeing one pilot bale out. Within minutes, as soon as the aircraft could be refuelled and rearmed, Duke was off again in company with Peter Olver leading, plus members of the Polish Team on a search of the area over which the air battle had taken place in the hope of sighting a dinghy or any sign of Gleed in the water. As Duke recorded at the time: 'We felt very sad and helpless after the action over Cap Bon and had to do something.'

They could not know that Gleed was beyond help. All they did know was that for them the war would continue. Although they missed The Widge they had to carry on without him.

Peter Olver took over command of 244 Wing and following a rest Neville Duke took command of 145 Squadron in Italy in 1944. He ended the war as one of Britain's top scoring fighter pilots. Olver was later shot down and taken prisoner over Italy and John Taylor, who had commanded 601 Squadron was killed in action over Sicily on 12 July 1943.

Ernst-Wilhelm Reinert was to end the war with 174 victories and Kommandor of IV/JG27. He received the Swords to his Knight's Cross on 1 February 1945. He ended the Tunisian campaign as the leading German fighter pilot with 51 victories claimed during those months before pulling out of Tunisia in May. Berres survived the campaign only to die in action over the Straits of Messina, Sicily, on 25 July 1943. Ironically enough he was escorting Ju52 transports and was attacked by 50 RAF fighters. He had gained a total of 53 victories and received a posthumous Knight's Cross. Bär survived the war with 220 victories including 16 kills claimed while flying the Messerschmitt 262 jet fighter during the last weeks of the war. He was killed in a light aeroplane crash at Brunswick on 28 April 1957.

Less than a month after Gleed died in action over Tunisia, the Axis forces surrendered. The battle for North Africa was over.

Epilogue

Doctor Seymour Gleed found the telegram lying on the door mat during morning surgery on Tuesday, 20 April. He knew what it would say without his having to open it. He and his wife and Daphne had lived for so long in the knowledge that one day that earth-shattering item might come. It was opened with extreme sadness, shock and an immense feeling of personal loss. Their son and brother was missing in action.

They had lived with the fear of this happening for so long, but had hoped that his vast experience, accumulated over nearly three years of active service, might somehow keep him safe. Yet they also knew that the longer he remained in action the greater his chance of his luck deserting him. For a time they held onto the slender thread that he was only 'missing' but as time went on without word they soon came to the realisation that Ian must be dead. Later his death was presumed officially.

It was recalled that Ian's childhood friend Reg Medlock was serving in North Africa. It was important now to be near Ian in death as they could no longer be with him in this life. Although eventually they might learn where his last resting place was, they wanted to know now as much as possible of his end and where he was. Doctor Gleed wrote to Reg Medlock in the hope that he could discover the whereabouts of Ian's grave.

The war in Tunisia and North Africa was now over. The guns were silent and the soldiers had moved on. Behind the scenes order slowly overcame disorder. The victors and the vanquished buried their dead, found their dead, reburied their dead.

Reg Medlock was a transport officer with the Royal Army Service Corps in Tunisia. He received the letter from Gleed's father informing him of Ian's loss, and that he had now heard that his aeroplane had come down at a place called Kefroab on Cap Bon.

(Actually he had come down at Zaduiet El M'Galz.) Reg Medlock had not seen his friend since 1940 but had followed his rise to fame with the RAF. This rise did not surprise him in the least knowing that Gleed was a person of great resource and initiative.

Medlock made two attempts at locating the crash site, the first one being frustrated by the sparsely populated countryside consisting of fields and sand dunes near the sea. On the second occasion he was fortunate in being able to enlist the help of an officer who spoke Arabic fluently and with his assistance they managed to contact a local villager who lived in the area and who was able to guide them to the exact location of the crashed Spitfire. Medlock relates:

> So far as I recall, the plane was more or less intact except for the engine which lay some few yards away. I looked for any traces of a body but was unable to find any signs except for a small piece of RAF uniform about two inches square. Neither could I find any trace of a grave, though evidently one was located later by the authorities.

Reg Medlock further remembers:

> The plane was lying among the sand dunes about 50 yards from the sea on the western coastline of Cap Bon. The position of the plane ... suggested that it had come down in a fairly flat approach and then hit the hummocks of the sand dunes. The piece of uniform suggests that (Gleed) may have been in the plane on crashing and perhaps thrown out. I don't think that there were any other signs of a personal nature in the wreckage of the plane and the piece of uniform was some few feet away from the plane.

Unable to find any trace or sign of a grave nearby, Medlock returned to the Spitfire and:

> I detached the panel bearing the [Figaro] mascot and sent it to Ian's parents. I also removed a plate which was fixed in the cockpit headed: – Engine Merlin XLV. Max Operational Limitations.

Who first discovered or reached the crash site is not known. Yet the location of the Spitfire and its appearance do suggest that Ian Gleed had tried to crash-land and was either dying or wounded while coming down or died in the attempt. What is known is that he was buried at Tazoghrane but was transferred and reburied at the Military Cemetary at Enfidaville just over one year later, on 25 April 1944, in Plot V, Row E, grave number 22. A simple cross marked his resting place, replaced in 1958 by the more familiar permanent headstone, of the type which can be seen in hundreds of military cemeteries all over Europe and the Middle East. The family had the opportunity to have any words of their choice put onto the stone. Gleed's mother chose these words by Robert Browning:

One who held
We fall to rise,
Are baffled to fight better,
Sleep to wake.

The Figaro marked panel taken from the Spitfire by Reg Medlock was received by the Gleed family and they kept it together with the two Hurricane cockpit doors similarly marked (see appendix E). In 1971 Gleed's sister, Doctor Daphne Gleed, generously donated them to the Royal Air Force Museum at Hendon for permanent display.

After the war the French Government honoured the memory of Wing Commander Ian Gleed with the posthumous award of the Croix de Guerre avec Etoile de Vermeil, gazetted on 5 June 1946.

Gleed's father died in 1950 and his wife followed him nine years later. Only Daphne remains, a charming and highly respected doctor. She fortunately has happy memories of her family, the dedicated doctor, a loving mother and a wonderful brother – 'Ian's life was short but he lived it to the full. To me he was a very dearly beloved brother and I was intensely proud of him and if possible become more so as time goes on.'

*

'I've grown up too fast. I want to be treated as if I were a
boy again; it is something I have lost, and I want it back.'

Appendices

Record of Service

Appointments and Promotions

Short Service Commission as Acting Pilot Officer on probation, General Duties. Branch RAF, with effect from 9 March 1936	4 May 1936
Graded as Pilot Officer	9 March 1937
Short Service Commission extended to 6 years	—
Flying Officer	9 October 1938
Acting Flight Lieutenant	7 November 1939
Relinquished a/F/Lt	18 February 1940
Acting Flight Lieutenant	11 May 1940
Flight Lieutenant	3 September 1940
Acting Squadron Leader	24 December 1940
Acting Wing Commander	18 November 1941
War Substantive Squadron Leader	18 February 1942
Transferred to Reserve & retained on Active List	9 March 1942
Death Presumed – Missing	16 April 1943

Postings

Civil Flying School, Filton	9 March 1936
RAF Depot (Uxbridge)	4 May 1936
8 Flying Training School, Montrose	16 May 1936
46 Squadron, Kenley & Digby	25 December 1936
266 Squadron, Sutton Bridge	7 November 1939
87 Squadron BEF France	14 May 1940
87 Squadron, Church Fenton, Exeter, Charmy Down	24 May 1940
RAF Station Middle Wallop	18 November 1941
HQ Fighter Command (Tactics)	16 July 1942
HQ Fighter Command (Operations)	7 December 1942
HQ RAF Middle East	1 January 1943
AHQ, RAF Western Desert	2 January 1943
HQ 244 Wing (to command)	31 January 1943

Wing Commander I.R. Gleed's combat victories 1940-43

Date	Type	Result	Remarks
18 May	Messerschmitt 110C	Destroyed	near Valenciennes
18 May	Messerschmitt 110C	Destroyed	near Valenciennes
19 May	Messerschmitt 109E	Probable	near Alost
19 May	Heinkel 111K	Destroyed	near Orchies, shared with Flying Officer Rayner
19 May	Dornier 17z	Destroyed	near Tournai
19 May	Dornier 17z	Destroyed	Valenciennes
19 May	Messerschmitt 109E	Destroyed	near Valenciennes
20 May	Junkers 88A	Destroyed	SE of Valenciennes, shared with PO Tait
15 Aug	Messerschmitt 110C	Destroyed	off Portland
15 Aug	Messerschmitt 110C	Destroyed	off Portland
15 Aug	Messerschmitt 109E	Probable	off Portland
25 Aug	Messerschmitt 110C	Destroyed	west of Portland
25 Aug	Messerschmitt 110C	Destroyed	west of Portland
25 Aug	Messerschmitt 109E	Damaged	south of Portland
30 Sep	Junkers 88A	Probable	south of Dorchester
1941			
7 May	Dornier 17z	Destroyed	mid-Channel
24 May	Dornier 18	Destroyed	Isle of Scilly, shared with Sgt Thorogood
28 May	Junkers 88	Probable	south of Scillies, shared with Flying Officer Watson
1942			
13 Mar	Junkers 88	Probable	near Alderney, shared with Pilot Officer Lynch
23 Mar	Junkers 88	Destroyed	off Portland
17 Apl	Messerschmitt 109F	Probable	Cherbourg, shared with Squadron Leader Currant
17 Apl	Messerschmitt 109F	Destroyed	Cherbourg
25 Apl	Messerschmitt 109F	Damaged	Cherbourg
5 May	Focke Wulf 190A	Probable	Hardelot

Date	*Type*	*Result*	*Remarks*
1943			
7 Mar	Messerschmitt 109F	Damaged	near Medinine
17 Mar	Messerschmitt 109G	Destroyed	east of German front line
6 Apl	Messerschmitt 109F	Damaged	near Cekmira

Aircraft claimed by Wing Commander Gleed during ground attacks

Date	*Type*	*Result*	*Remarks*
1941			
15 Mar	Dornier 17z	Destroyed	Caen, shared with Flight Lieutenant Rayner
15 Mar	Dornier 17z	Damaged	Caen aerodrome
15 Mar	Junkers 88	Damaged	Caen aerodrome
6 Aug	Messerschmitt 109F	Damaged	Maupertus aerodrome
6 Aug	Messerschmitt 109F	Damaged	Maupertus aerodrome

Ian Gleed's Decorations

Award promulgated in the London Gazette 13 September 1940

DISTINGUISHED FLYING CROSS

Flight Lieutenant Ian Richard Gleed (37800) Royal Air Force

Flight Lieutenant Gleed took over a flight in No 87 Squadron on arriving from England after intensive hostilities had begun. The Squadron was moved several times, and he knew neither the officers nor the airmen. He took on his task with energy and discretion, won the confidence of his flight and led them with skill and success. In his very first patrol his flight was engaged by greatly superior numbers of enemy fighters and he accounted for 2 Me110s. Throughout he showed great courage in the air and was on duty almost continuously.

*

Award promulgated in the London Gazette 22 May 1942

DISTINGUISHED SERVICE ORDER

Wing Commander Ian Richard Gleed DFC (37800) Royal Air Force

This officer has led his Wing on 26 sorties over enemy territory. He has always displayed a fine fighting spirit which combined with his masterly leadership and keenness has set an inspiring example. Wing Commander Gleed has destroyed at least 12 enemy aircraft, two of which he shot down at night.

*

CROIX DE GUERRE BELGE

Awarded 15 February 1943
Promulgated in the London Gazette 9 April 1943

A senior officer of great bravery and outstanding competence. The leader of a unit of several Belgian pilots, he led them in battle through several offensives over enemy occupied territory, inspiring them with the example of his drive and devotion to duty.

*

CROIX DE GUERRE FRANCAIS
AVEC ETOILE DE VERMEIL

Promulgated in the London Gazette 5 June 1946

APPENDIX D

Aeroplanes flown by Ian Gleed

De Havilland Tiger Moth	London Aeroplane Club, Hatfield.	G-ADLU G-ADWB	1st Solo on type November 16, 1935
De Havilland Gipsy Moth	,, 1935-36	G-ABHN	
Hawker Hart Hawker Audax Hawker Fury	No 8 FTS, Montrose, 1936		
Gloster Gauntlet Gloster Gauntlet II	46 Squadron Kenley & Digby 1937-38, B Flight	K5282 K5272 K5274 K5275 K5286 K5316 K5317 K5321 K7794 K7843 K7845 K7851 K7860 K7891	Gleed's usual machine. Empire Air Day display May 28, 1938
Miles M14 Magister	,,	L5940 P6346	June 1938 June 1939
Hawker Hurricane I	46 Squadron Digby	L1567 L1791	1st on type November 19, 1938 Collected from Brooklands Feb 6, 1939

	1938-40 B Flight	L1794	Collected from Brooklands Feb 6, 1939
		L1795	Collected from Northolt Feb 10, 1939
		L1796	Collected from Brooklands Feb 7, 1939
		L1803	
		L1804	Empire Air Day display May 20, 1939
		L1806	
		L1807	
		L1813	
		L1817	
		L1857	
Bristol Blenheim I	266 Squadron, Sutton Bridge 1940, B Flight	L6686 L6694	1st on type November 7, 1939
Miles Master	,,	N3162 N3165	
Miles Magister	,,	N3867 P2458	November 1939 May 1940
Fairey Battle I	,,	L5031 L5242 L5248 L5268 L5330 L5350 L5368 L5369 L5374 L5375	
Supermarine Spitfire I	,,	N3120 N3175	Collected from Brize Norton Jan 20, 1940 Test flight February 18, 1940. Machine broke up in air, Gleed descended by parachute.
Hawker Hurricane I	87 Squadron France, Exeter & Charmy Down, 1940-41,	P2798	Coded LK-A 'Figaro' Gleed's usual machine May 1940-August 1941. Destroyed 2 Me110s May 18, 1940 Probable Me109 May 19, 1940

A Flight & Commander		Destroyed He111 May 19, 1940
		Destroyed 2 Do17s May 19, 1940
		Destroyed Me109 May 19, 1940
		Destroyed Ju88 May 20, 1940
		Destroyed 2 Me110s August 15, 1940
		Probable Me109 August 15, 1940
		Destroyed 2 Me110s August 25, 1940
		Damaged Me109 August 25, 1940
		Probable Ju88 September 30, 1940
		Destroyed Do17 May 7, 1941
		Probable Ju88 May 28, 1941
		Intruder sortie March 14/15, 1941 – Destroyed Do17 on ground, Damaged Do17 on ground, Damaged Ju88 on ground
	P3093	
	P3118	
	P3289	June 1941
	P3404	Coded LK-J Patrol July 8, 1940
	P3527	June 1941
	P3755	Coded LK-Z July 1940
	V7136	
	V7204	Coded LK-V Three patrols July 1940
	W9154	Coded LK-D Night Patrol May 10, 1941
	W9173	Coded LK-V Dropped bombs on enemy airfield May 6, 1941
	W9196	Coded LK-B Destroyed Do18 May 24, 1941
Supermarine Spitfire I	P9490	June 20, 1940
Hawker Hurricane II	Z3224	July 1941
	Z3527	June 1941
	Z3576	June 1941
	Z3591	June 1941
	Z3774	July 1941
	Z3775	
	Z3779	Coded LK-A 'Figaro' July-November 1941. Attacked Maupertus aerodrome August 6,1941.
	BE500	November 1941
Miles Magister	R1825	
De Havilland Tiger Moth	N6932	

Supermarine Spitfire Vb/Vc	Middle Wallop & Ibsley Wings 1941-42	W3946	November 1941
		AA729	May 1942
		AA742	Coded IR-G 'Figaro' November 1941-May 1942 Flew 'Veracity' ops December 18 and 30, 1941 Flew over 'Channel Dash' February 12, 1942 Probable Ju88 March 13, 1942 Destroyed Ju88 March 23, 1942 Destroyed Me109 April 17, 1942 Probable Me109 April 17, 1942 Damaged Me109 April 25, 1942
		AA747	November 1941
		AB380	April/May 1942. Flew ops on: April 30, May 1, June 1, 3, 4 & 26.
		AB514	Flew op. May 18, 1942
		AR274	Probable FW190 May 5, 1942
		AR372	Roadstead op. May 15, 1942
		BL974	March/April 1942
		BP862	Flew op. May 9, 1942
		BR160	July 1942
		EN956	Flew op. June 20, 1942
Hawker Hurricane I		P3961	Cannon test June 18, 1942
Miles Magister		L8321	
		N3902	
		R1914	
Supermarine Spitfire Vb/Vc	145 Squadron (attached) North Africa Jan/Feb 1943	EP309	February 14/15, 1943
		EP550	Escort to Malta February 18, 1943
		ER170	Mid-February 1943
		ER650	Flew at least 7 ops. January 16-22, 1943
Supermarine Spitfire Vb/Vc	244 Wing Desert Air Force, 1943	EP543	February 1943
		EP966	Recce: sortie March 6, 1943
		ER170	ex 145 machine – Coded IR-G 'Figaro' February 1943.
		ER549	Flew op. February 27, 1943
		ER622	Flew op. March 10, 1943

Spitfire IX	,,	EN186	Flew ops. March 26 & 28, 1943
		EN261	Flew ops. April 6, 7 & 8, 1943
Spitfire Vb	,,	AB502	Coded IR-G 'Figaro'

Spitfire Vb   ,,   AB502   Coded IR-G 'Figaro'
At least 35 operations flown between
March-April 1943.
Damaged Me109 March 7, 1943
Destroyed Me109 March 17, 1943
Damaged Me109 April 6, 1943
Shot down in combat April 16, 1943

Aeroplane Types flown by Ian Gleed 1935-43

De Havilland Tiger Moth
De Havilland Gipsy Moth
De Havilland Hornet Moth
Hawker Hart
Hawker Audax
Hawker Fury
Gloster Gauntlet II
Gloster Gladiator
Miles Magister
Hawker Hurricane I

Bristol Blenheim
Supermarine Spitfire I
Miles Master
Hawker Hurricane II
Bell Airacobra
Supermarine Spitfire Vb/Vc
Vickers Wellington
Supermarine Spitfire IX
Fairey Battle I

Figaro(s)

Ian Gleed's Figaro mascot which he had painted by the cockpits of his Hurricanes and Spitfires became well known and quickly associated with the pilot of those aeroplanes.

There is no certain evidence that he had the painting on any machines prior to his joining 87 Squadron although if he didn't it seems strange that he should do so immediately he joined an active squadron who were in the middle of a very active war.

P2798 Gleed took over the brand new ex-factory Hurricane the day after his arrival in France – 17 May 1940. It had left the factory of the Gloster Aircraft Company, having been built under licence, at the end of March 1940 and taken on charge by No 20 Maintenance Unit on 5 April. The Figaro cat motif was painted on the Hurricane's removable cockpit door, situated on the starboard side of the Hurricane. The cat was black and white with yellow iris and black pupils. Its right paw (and possibly its tail) was hitting (or zapping) a German swastika. This swastika, shattering under the blow, was painted grey. There was red blood painted to the tips of the right paw with two blood drips immediately under the claw.

Gleed flew this machine almost constantly from 17 May 1940 until 4 August 1941 – a remarkably long period for an operational aeroplane. During this time the machine was repainted either in part or in total at least twice. The first time was in early 1941 when it was painted black for night flying duties but was later restored to its day camouflage of green and brown. During these changes, the Figaro marking was left intact although the swastika and blood drips were painted out then replaced. When Gleed took command of 87 Squadron he had a squadron leader's pennant painted on the port side of the cockpit just under the windscreen, with '87' painted on the bottom right hand corner of it.

When Gleed flew the demonstration flight against a Curtiss P40 Tomahawk – in which the Hurricane could out-manoeuvre and turn inside – on 6 February 1941, several pictures were taken of P2798 in its dark paint. These pictures show a blue nose marking which reached back to and below the engine exhaust stubs. There was also two similar blue horizontal stripes painted on the rudder. These blue markings were not replaced when day camouflage was re-applied.

P2798's individual markings were LK-A, the 'A' being forward of the

British RAF roundel on both sides of the fuselage. When the Airfix plastic model kit manufacturers introduced a 1/24th scale model of the Hawker Hurricane Mark I, it depicted Gleed's famous aeroplane.

Immediately after Gleed stopped flying P2798 it was flown by other 87 Squadron pilots. Sergeants Castle, Thompson and Gibbs flew it during September and October 1941 on interceptions and from the Scillies. Its last flight on operations occurred on 3 October, when Sergeant Gibbs flew an interception mission. It was finally struck off charge on 1 November. The cockpit door was retained by Ian Gleed and kept by his family after his death.

Z3779   Gleed flew this Kingston built Hurricane on 3 July 1941 and soon it became his regular mount for the rest of his time with 87 Squadron; to November 1941. The cockpit door of this Hurricane was marked with a new painting of Figaro. It was very similar to the original except that the 'zapping' paw was totally coloured blood red, as was the tip of the cat's tail. There was an increase in blood drips – nine, and the swastika was white with red shatter marks. Code letters remained LK-A and the squadron leader's pennant located by the cockpit on the port side. The door of this machine was also retained by Gleed and later by his family.

AA742   This Spitfire Vb was the one Gleed used as his personal machine as Ibsley Wing leader until the end of April 1942. It was coded with his personal initials IR-G and carried a wing commander's pennant painted by the windscreen on both the port and starboard sides. Figaro was also painted on the starboard side.

AB380 & AR274   These Spitfire Vbs were the two usual machines flown by Ian Gleed as Wing Leader during the summer of 1942. AB380 being the most used. It is fairly certain that both these carried Figaro painted on the starboard side by the cockpit. At least one Figaro was painted on a pale blue square, located under the cockpit rim. There was less blood, just a suggestion of this on Figaro's right paw. The swastika was probably painted red, edged in white.

ER170   Gleed flew several different Spitfires with 145 Squadron in North Africa but it is unlikely any were marked with his initials until he officially took over as Wing Leader in February 1943. ER170 was probably the first machine in North Africa he had marked with IR-G, painted in red and outlined in yellow. Figaro was painted under the cockpit on the starboard side, still zapping a swastika, this time coloured white and rather more shattered than previously. An innovation to associate Figaro with North Africa was that the broken swastika was crashing into and breaking a black coloured palm tree. Unfortunately, after his groundcrew had gone to the trouble of painting all this onto ER170 he only flew it on a very few occasions before he took over AB502.

AB502 A modified Spitfire Vb with clipped wings. An ex-145 Squadron aeroplane it was taken over by Gleed in early March 1943 and was flown on at least 35 missions. Figaro was again painstakingly painted onto the fuselage together with his wing commander's pennant on the port side and his IR-G in red and yellow, the 'G' being behind the roundel on the port side, forward of it on the starboard side. There appears to be no blood on Figaro and the swastika was white, the palm tree black. The Figaro motif from AB502 was taken from the crashed Spitfire and returned to Gleed's parents. This plus the two Hurricane doors were donated to the RAF Museum by Gleed's sister in 1971.

Bibliography

Arise to Conquer Ian Gleed, Victor Gollancz Ltd, 1942
Public School Explorers in Newfoundland Dennis Clarke, Putnam, 1935
Young Pioneers in Northern Finland G. Murray Levick, PSES, 1934
Strictly Personal W. Somerset Maugham, Willliam Heinemann Ltd, 1942
A Penguin in the Eyrie Hector Bolitho, Hutchinson, 1955
Fighters over Tunisia C.F. Shores, H. Ring & W.N. Hess, Spearman, 1975
Aces High C.F. Shores & C. Williams, Spearman, 1966
The Flying Sailor André Jubelin, Hurst & Blackett, 1953
Test Pilot Neville Duke, Allan Wingate, Ltd, 1953
Against the Sun Edward Lanchbery, Cassell & Co Ltd, 1955
Phoenix into Ashes Roland Beamont, W. Kimber & Co, 1968
RAF Year Book 1938 compiled by Leonard Bridgman, Gale & Polden, 1938
Night Intruder J. Howard-Williams, David & Charles Ltd, 1976
The Flying Sword Tom Moulson, MacDonald, 1964
Polish Wings in the West Bohdan Arct, Interpress, 1971
2 Group RAF M.J.F. Bowyer, Faber & Faber, 1974
Twenty One Squadrons Leslie Hunt, Garnstone Press, 1972
87 Squadron History 1917-61 N.L.R. Frank, Unpublished MS
'Widge' – The story of W/C I.R. Gleed DSO DFC.' Article by Chaz
    Bowyer *Aircraft Illustrated*, Aug 1971.

Index

Names and Places

German Luftwaffe Squadrons

Royal Air Force Squadrons

South African Air Force Squadrons

USAAF Units

Groups, Wings and Flights of the RAF

Allied Aeroplanes

Axis Aeroplanes